Travel and Teaching in
Portugal
and
Spain
A Photographic Journey

Mark J. Curran

Order this book online at www.trafford.com
or email orders@trafford.com

Most Trafford titles are also available at major online book retailers.

Printed in the United States of America.

ISBN: 978-1-4907-3211-4 (sc)
ISBN: 978-1-4907-3212-1 (e)

Trafford rev. 04/02/2014

Trafford PUBLISHING® www.trafford.com

North America & international
toll-free: 1 888 232 4444 (USA & Canada)
fax: 812 355 4082

I dedicate this book first of all to my wife Keah and daughter Katie who enriched the journey and put up with the sometimes rough spots during travel, and secondarily, to Dr. Michael Flys (deceased) and his wife Felisa and daughter Tamara who guided us in Spain and provided many fun moments. "Gracias a todos!"

Table of Contents

List of Images

PREFACE

In 2014 as I continue in retirement to write the teaching-research-travel books (the series already treats Brazil, Colombia, Guatemala and Mexico) I return to an endeavor of many years ago in 1987, one that cannot be left out of the total images and classes taught at A.S.U.—the trip to Portugal and Spain.

The trip was over several months in 1987 and involved three facets:

1. My first visit to the "Metrópoli" of Portugal. After all the years teaching Portuguese language, the Brazilian version, and diverse courses on Brazilian Literature and Civilization and a one-time graduate reading course on Portugal's master work "The Lusiads" by Luís de Camões, there was finally an opportunity to visit much of Portugal. This phase of travel in 1987 was prior to the main purpose of the trip . . .

2. A two-month sojourn in Spain teaching in the Arizona State University Summer School under the direction of Dr. Michael Flys, my chair in the Department of Languages and Literatures. This would involve a first phase of teaching in Málaga and visits to the principal cultural sites of Andalucía, a wonderful travel phase to the main parts of central, north and northwest old Spain, and a second phase of teaching in Madrid with local trips to the area.

3. There was for the Currans a final short religious "pilgrimage" to the "Sanctuaries" which brought many pleasant surprises in northern Spain and France.

An unusual aspect of these travels for me was that it really was a family affair. My wife Keah and young nine-year-old daughter Katie were present the entire time. So the dynamics were a lot different than my solo trips to Brazil and my trips with Keah to Brazil, Colombia and then Guatemala and Mexico prior to Katie's arrival in 1977.

There were many happy, memorable things shared, albeit with a few bumps in the road as well. When I look back, I would not trade the experience. Michael Flys made possible a new event in life for us. He ran one of the most efficient and quality summer schools in Spain by any university in the United States. And secondly he provided the means for us to really get to know a large part of Spain.

Once again, like the case of Portugal, I was a late-comer to Spain, ironically in a way. When I was applying for grants for graduate school while at Rockhurst College in Kansas City, Missouri, in 1963, I applied for a Fulbright Grant to Spain since that was the place highest on my list to continue study in Spanish language and literature (I had a minor in Spanish at Rockhurst). I did not win the grant but was offered a second choice in Mexico. At that time I had no major interest or even preparation for a Ph.D. level topic in Mexico, so I applied to Saint Louis University for their Ph.D. program in Spanish and Latin American Studies with a minor in Luso-Brazilian Studies. The rest is history: three years of graduate study in Saint Louis where I majored in Spanish and "Siglo de Oro," then to Brazil for research on the "literatura de cordel" and its relation to erudite Brazilian Literature. And finally there was the teaching career at Arizona State University. I am getting around to the analogy with Portuguese. After a long career of thirty-four years full time and nine years part time of teaching Spanish Language, Introduction to Spanish Literature, Civilization of Spain, and the one-time course on "Don Quixote" at ASU, I finally made it to the "metrópoli."

So Portugal and Spain came late, but not unimportantly. I had learned my lessons in history and literature, and this trip preceded by much study and preparation truly "filled in the gaps" of a teaching career.

So to begin, I once again thank Dr. Michael Flys (now deceased) and his wife Felisa and daughter Tamara for having us. I repaid the favor with CDs of all the photos taken in Spain as a gift to them. I think Michael and Felisa truly appreciated them and in short visits to an ailing Michael before his death I believe we had good final encounters. I'm hoping this book will continue to repay the favor.

So let's tell the story! It enables me to go back in time and recall the wonderful sights of Portugal and Spain as well as see the highlights of their cultures. The many photos illustrating this book stand as proof. One note: this was my/our first trip to Europe. My only base of comparison was extensive travel in the New World; therefore one notes my occasional references to Mexico City, Guatemala, Colombia and especially to Portugal's colony of Brazil.

The notes as to the classes I taught in Spain will be limited. In all honesty it was what went on outside the classroom that mattered, and that is the main part of the narrative in Spain. The text will follow loosely the format of a diary, that is, with some of the dates of travel. But each stop on the trip will be documented for its history and importance.

PART ONE

THE PORTUGAL ODYSSEY

May 27

International Travel from Phoenix to New York to Lisbon on TWA

Travel from Phoenix to New York's Kennedy was uneventful; the NYC airport seemed old, dirty and run down. Significant on this trip was the time change: a total of eight hours difference between Phoenix and Lisbon. The plane left Kennedy at 6:30 p.m. EDT and arrived in Lisbon at 6:30 a.m. We saw the sunset in New York and the sunrise in Lisbon.

There was an interesting conversation on board with an elderly gentleman from Barcelona who fought with Generalísimo Francisco Franco in the Spanish Civil War, but had two brothers on the other side! This confirms common knowledge of the times: a Spain truly divided. Franco of course was supported by Hitler, Mussolini and the Axis; the Left by Russia. It was Fascist versus Communist-Anarchist sympathizers, family members and relatives on different sides and in many cases Catholics versus a church-clergy-hating Left. There were vestiges of this in our own Department of Foreign Languages at Arizona State University—extreme Catholics alongside atheist anti-Franco folks. But I thought this encounter was significant as a preamble to Spain.

Another conversation on board revealed an interesting facet of academic life if you read between the lines. We met a marine biologist from landlocked South Dakota State University on a fifteen month sabbatical to study the animals on the beaches of Portugal!

PREAMBLE TO PORTUGAL AND LISBON: THEIR HISTORY

Metropolitan Lisbon has over three million in population and the old city center has some 550,000. It is the westernmost large city located in Europe lying on the western Iberian Peninsula on the Atlantic Ocean and the River Tagus.

An interesting tourist note is that it is the seventh-most-visited city in Southern Europe after Istanbul, Rome, Barcelona, Madrid, Athens and Milan. I understand that it is the oldest city in Western Europe predating London, Paris and Rome by hundreds of years. Julius Caesar made it a "municipium" with the name "Olissipo." After the fall of Rome it was ruled by Germanic tribes from the 5th century, captured by the Moors in the 8th century and was reconquered by Bergundian King Afonso Henriques and the Crusaders in 1147. The city grew as Portugal's capital and as the Portuguese expeditions of the Age of Discovery left from Lisbon during the 15th to 16th centuries. The 15th and 16th centuries were its "Golden Age" with discovery and commerce in Africa, India, the Far East and later on Brazil. The Manueline style of architecture of that period predominated in the Tower of Belem and the Jerónimos Monastery.

After the debacle of King Sebastian and his utopic battle against the Moors in Morocco and his subsequent death in 1578, the crown was left vacant and in the succession crisis Spain came to rule Portugal in 1580. The Restoration took place sixty years later in 1640 with the Avis Dynasty in place. The House of Avis continued its rule until the earth shattering, literally, earthquake of 1755 which destroyed a large part of Lisbon. It would be rebuilt by Sebastião José de Carvalho e Melo, the 1st Marquis of Pombal.

The next important time was the invasion of Portugal by Napoleon Bonaparte in the 19th century forcing the Bragança Queen Maria I and Prince-Regent João VI to flee with the royal family to Brazil. This is the only time in modern history of Europe when the home country is ruled from its colony! After Napoleon's defeat the royal family returned, minus Pedro I who decided to remain in Brazil (Brazilianists recall his "I am staying" ["Eu fico"] speech) and established a constitutional monarchy there until the forced abdication of the Braganças in 1889.

The Braganças then ruled in Portugal until 1908 with the regicide of Carlos I and the advent of the First Republic.

The next great moment was the "Estado Novo" of much of the twentieth century under Salazar and his death followed by the Revolution of the Flowers in 1974 bringing the Portuguese Third Republic.

ARRIVAL AND TOURISM IN LISBON

All did not begin too well in Lisbon. We did ride in a Mercedes-Benz taxi for $3.00 to a small hotel that had not received our reservation, but we managed a tiny, uncomfortable room and beds. Exhausted, we dropped the bags and had our first Portuguese breakfast, curiously to me called "pequeno almoço" which consisted of bread, butter, jam and not so tasty coffee ("almoço" in Brazil is the huge midday meal). The place was called the "Residência Dublin."

"A Praça dos Restauradores," Lisbon

We were in a state of jet lag as we headed to Lisbon's main avenue, I understand modeled after the main avenues of Paris; "Avenida da Liberdae," with its beautiful trees and cafés links the "Praça dos Restauradores" to the "Praça de Pombal." The avenue is broad with many lanes of traffic and long broad sidewalks with gardens along their sides. The avenue evolved from the "Passeio Público" from 1764 and was modeled after the Boulevards of Paris; it soon had the palaces of the most weathy families of Lisbon along its side. These have been replaced by office buildings, hotels and cinemas (we saw advertisements for a Charles Bronson adventure film), but still there are statues remembering the height of Portuguese literary history with figures of the age like Almeida Garrett, Alexandre Herculano and others. It is the scene of the largest parade in Lisbon with the night of St. Anthony of Lisbon.

"Monumento ao Marquês de Pombal"

The monument is dedicated to the "Marquês de Pombal" Sebastião José de Carvalho e Melo, the prime minister who ruled Portugal from 1750 to 1777. He is most beloved by the Portuguese by virtue of rebuilding Lisbon after the devastating earthquake of 1755, justly so. But for me he was the leader of Portugal who among other things would reign at the time of the decree throwing the Jesuit Order out of Brazil and Spanish America as well in 1767. Without some serious research and many pages of prose, horribly involved stuff, one cannot know the whys and wherefores of all this. But for the Brazilians and "Brazilianists" and people who admire the Jesuits, he gets a black mark. From the times of Padre Antônio Vieira who preached to the Indians in North Eastern Brazil, to the Jesuits who wrote the first Portuguese Grammar Book in Brazil, to the countless Jesuits who brought Christianity to the natives of Brazil, in particular to the "Missões" in the South, all was lost with Pombal's decree. The Order had to leave the premises, almost, as it were, "overnight." Schools, hospitals and missions were left to the Crown to designate to other religious orders. It took a long while for Brazil to recover. One needs to see the film "The Mission" with Robert de Niro and Jeremy Irons to get an idea of the devastating consequences for the natives of southern Brazil. The Jesuits were allowed to return, albeit in a most modest fashion, and with the Second Vatican Council and its aftermath, play a much different role in today's Brazil. They espoused the "church of the poor" and much of the theology of Liberation Theology and are champions of the cause of poor Brazilians yet today. A person cognizant of their thinking is current Pope Francis, a Jesuit himself.

We then hopped a bus to Rossio Plaza the main transportation hub of Lisbon with the trains heading out to all corners of Portugal. One of the main squares of Lisbon since the Middle Age, it is a center of popular life in Lisbon as well as its Rossio Train Station. It was the place of the Portuguese Inquisition and there were public executions in the plaza in the 16th Century. Two centuries later after the earthquake the writer Romantic writer Almeida Garrett convinced all to build the Portuguese National Theater where the Inquisition building had been destroyed, the Teatro Maria Isabel. But back in the 16th century it later had been a meeting place for the Portuguese to conspire against Spain and its control of Portugal from 1580 (King Sebastião was killed in Morocco and with no hereditary leader, by blood it all passed to Spain and Felipe II) to 1640 and the famous Restoration marked by yet another monument on Avenida da Liberdade. As mentioned, our practical connection to the Square was the Rossio Train Station which was built in 1886 in Neo-Manueline Architecture. On that enormous first day in Lisbon it was difficult to absorb it all; it felt like when I landed as a young bachelor set to do Ph.D. research in Rio de Janeiro in 1966 and was overwhelmed by the immensity of the city.

View of "Rio Tejo" and "Praça do Comércio"

Blue Tile "Azulejos"—Old Scene of "Praça do Comércio"

We walked through the busy commercial center of Lisbon on the "mosaic sidewalks" like those in Rio to the port's main plaza, the "Praça do Comércio" or "A Praça do Paço." It faced the famous and impressive Tagus River with a huge bridge to the right or north and a Christ figure across the river. It was replete with large ocean liners, navy and cargo ships and many ferries.

Originally known as the "Terreiro do Paço" or Palace Square because it was the place of the Royal Ribeira Palace, it was later to be destroyed in the earthquake of 1755 and rebuilt as the "Praça do Comércio" by the Marquês de Pombal. It had been King Manuel of the Avis Dynasty who had built the Ribeira Palace in the early 16th century (the time of the "Manuelino" architecture throughout Lisbon and Belém). The original plaza had housed the "Casa da Índia" regulating commerce with that part of the world after the discoveries of Vasco da Gama in 1497 (related to the similar purpose of the "Casa de Contratación" of Spain in Sevilla). It contains a great arch and the first statue of a Portuguese King in Lisbon after the earthquake which highlights the Praça. A more gloomy fact is that it also was the place where the next to last King of Portugal, Carlos I, was assassinated in 1908. Only two years later the Republicans overthrew the Portuguese monarchy.

While serenely gazing down to the river we noted several men of very poor appearance up to their knees in the mud and muck digging large worms for fishing bait ["gusanos de isca"]. The tide was out and there was a foul smell close to the water. The overflowing worm buckets were a bit disgusting that first morning in Lisbon.

We then wandered through the "Passeio Público" going from the "Praça do Comércio" into the busy city center. Eventually we ended back at the Rossio with an unusual first lunch in Portugal: "pregos"—meat and bread sandwiches—and "croks"—ice creams. Still in a state of shock and learning about Portugal, we would not adapt to the big noon meal until a bit later.

We returned to Avenida da Liberdade with its nice walkways past the Rossio Station with its Manueline architectural style and past "Restauradores" Monument marking Portugal's independence from Spain in 1640. We recall once again that Spain came to rule Portugal in 1580 as a consequence of the death of Portuguese King Sebastião of the House of Avis who had embarked on an utopist mission to carry the conquest of the Moors into northern Africa where he met his end. But the year of 1640 brought an end that was not so clear cut; Portugal and Spain were at each other's throats for many years, but the culmination was the rule of the House of Bragança until the 20th century and the end of it all.

One needs to remember that this trip was my first to the "Old World," and dates and history would be important.

Exhausted Katie was in shock and tears in the p.m.; Keah and I were not far from it. We adopted the motto, "We are building character. A little suffering is good." Katie was a real trooper later in the p.m. Why this suffering? We all found it impossible to sleep with the time change. We did return to our room, a very depressing place at first, but then felt a bit better after a two or three hour nap. It was bad jet lag; we basically had been up all night.

View of Lisbon from the "Bairro Alto"

In better spirits after the nap, but just a bit, and the unexpected icy showers in the inhospitable Residência Dublin, we took a taxi to the "Bairro Alto" with its view of the city. Built from the old city walls of Lisbon, it gradually developed in importance. The arrival of the Jesuits in 1540 and the establishement of São Roque Church was an important time. In modern times it became known for the "Fado" cafés, the Largo de Camões, Rua Garret and the bar-restaurant "A Brazileira" famous for its clients like the 20th century genius poet, Fernando Pessoa. This café-tea shop-bar-restaurant is one of the oldest and most famous cafés in the old quarter of Lisbon located at 120 Rua Garrett at one end of the Largo do Chiado near the Baixa-Chiado Metro Stop. It started in 1905 by selling "genuine Brazilian coffee" from the state of Minas Gerais. It was the first shop to sell the "bica", a small cup of strong coffee like Brazil's "cafezinho." It was at the "Brazileira" we were introduced to the "bica." Its most famous client was the great 20th century poet Fernando Pessoa whose bronze statue is placed outside the place. It reminded me very much of the "Confeitaria Colombo" and its elegance in Rio de Janeiro.

Shopping in the "Chiado" district

This part of Lisbon has been inhabited since Roman times! North European Crusaders later settled in the area during the Siege of Lisbon in 1147. Prosperity followed and then disaster; the 1755 earthquake did minimal damage but a huge fire in the late 1980s did far more. But it has been rebuilt as a popular shopping area.

We ended that p.m. once again in the "Chiado" Shopping area, not too far from the "Rossio" and "Restauradores," and found our "hangout" ("ponto" as they say in Brazil)—the "Bom Jardim" Restaurant and our first meal - delicious Portuguese style barbecued chicken ["frango grelhado"]. The restaurant was actually in the bar district ["cervejaria"] of central Lisbon. Keah and I were introduced to delicious "Vinho Verde," a light wine with just a bit of carbonation, the brand name "Gatão," and pastries. That improved all our dispositions. Back at the "Residência Dublin" we did travel diaries (thanks to those notes I can do this book) and to bed.

Musing on that first day's experience I wrote: Lisbon is historically more interesting than Rio, but appears old and poor with many street beggars. Twenty-seven years later our daughter Katie told me it was the street beggars that made the biggest impression on her (at the age of nine) and in a way influenced her as an adult to make her first documentary film on the poor farmers of the world, including those in Cuba, Mexico, Brazil, Africa, India and the Native American Tribes. It was strange to note at the airport all the flights from Angola and Mozambique and strange to see the all black airline crews, a first for the "gringo."

I noted all the graffiti along street walls, much of it by the P.C.P., "Partido Comunista Português," and we walked by the Socialist Party Headquarters. These things you did not see in Brazil.

I was pleased with the communicating in Portugal, almost no problems at all with my Brazilian Portuguese. The Portuguese think we are from southern Brazil! The magic words "speak slowly please ["fale devagar por favor"] solved most everything.

May 29th.

View across Lisbon to the "Castelo de São Jorge"

We began the day with coffee on the "terrace" of the Dublin; there is continuing delightful spring weather, a bit cool but with sunshine. This time the "café com leite" was accompanied by delicious bread. Then it was off to the "Castelo de São Jorge."

"O Castelo de São Jorge"—History

It was originally a Moorish castle occupying a hilltop overlooking the old historic center of Lisbon and the Tagus River. Prior to that time it had roots in Celtic tribes, Phoenicians, Greeks, Carthaginians and the Romans. With the fall of Rome, the "Suevos" and Visigoths ruled before the Moors. With the Christian "Reconquista" by Afonso Henriques and the Knights of the Second Crusade the siege of Lisbon took place in 1147 and the Christians took Lisbon. The Castle was later named "São Jorge" after the Pact with the English in 1371. The latter were important allies of the Portuguese in 1385 and the Battle of Aljubarrota in effect freeing Portugal from Spanish dominion. We were told this is the oldest political alliance in Europe. When Lisbon became the center of the Kingdom in 1255, the Castelo de São Jorge became the fortified residence of King Afonso III, was later renovated by King Dinis in 1300 and became the Royal Palace of the Alcáçova. The castle resisted the advances of Spain in the 14th century and was finally dedicated to King João I and his wife Filipa of Lancaster. Later the castle was the setting for the reception of the return of Vasco da Gama from India in 1498. It was a theater for the plays of Gil Vicente. It began its decline in the 16th century when the Portuguese built a new palace along the Tagus River in Belém, a "suburb" of Lisbon along the Tagus reaching to the open Atlantic. The decline continued during the Spanish rule and finally with much destruction by the earthquake of 1755. Salazar in the 20th century sponsored its rebuilding and it is a major tourist site today.

Side View of "Castelo de São Jorge"

We took a taxi to the "Castelo de São Jorge" one of the landmarks of Lisbon. It was my first European castle! From the parapet one has a fine view of the Rio Tejo, the Alfama district and the rest of the city.

The Walk through the "Alfama"

A Street in the "Alfama" District—Laundry Hanging from the Balconies

It is the oldest district of Lisbon, between the "Castelo de São Jorge" and the "Rio Tejo." The name comes from the Arabic "fountains or baths." During the time of the Moors it constituted the entire city of Lisbon; it later became the main aristocratic part of the city, but much later was inhabited by the fishermen and other poor "Lisboetas" and remains that way today. It escaped the earthquake of 1755 so remains largely intact. The "miradouros" or overlooks to the Tagus are impressive as is the nearby beginning of the Lisbon trolley or "elétrico" and the Museum of Portuguese Tiles or "Azulejos."

Ice Cream at a "Botequim" in the "Alfama"

Since many buildings of the "Alfama" were not affected by the horrendous earthquake of 1755, it maintins its old appearance. From the nearby Belvedere of the "Largo de São Salvador" we saw once again the view of the river and beyond. The streets are cobblestone and the sidewalks are "pedradas," stones smooth from wear and slippery. The Alfama was all very quaint with narrow winding streets and lots of "becos" or dead end alleyways as well. The balconies were replete with flowers and the streets with lots of stray dogs. It had more character than some other parts of the city, and yet the latter were not far behind. The famous balconies all had the laundry out, a trait of the Alfama.

The old ladies at the Residênca Dublin including the manager all warned of street thieves in the Alfama, but one shop owner said the thieves "get only little old women." There were many typical cafés, and some "tascas" or bars. We did see one or two "varinas," the fish monger ladies dressed all in black with boots on and busy cleaning fish. There were one or two "fado" restaurants but I understand the "Bairro Alto" is better known for this. The Alfama seemed almost free of cars and traffic, very nice.

The "Museu de Azulejos"

"Façada" of the "Museu dos Azulejos"

Portugal is most famous for these tiles which it took to its many colonies-possesions, including to Brazil (you see them especially in the colonial churches of the North East, like the convents of Olinda or Recife or the "Igreja de São Francisco" in Salvador), so this had to be an important part of Lisbon for me. The custom was inherited from the Moorish tradition but found a true home in Portugal where outstanding examples can be found throughout the nation. We have out of necessity limited the images to one or two examples, but the museum itself was outstanding, a beautiful example of art and culture in Lisbon and Portugal.

Portuguese Tile Scene "Museu dos Azulejos" 1

Portuguese Tile Scene "Museu dos Azulejos" 2

The Cathedral of Lisbon [Ireja da Sé]

Cathedral of Lisbon—"Igreja da Sé"

Its official name is "The Patriarchal Cathedral of St. Mary Major of Lisbon." It was begun by Afonso Henriques in 1147 and has been modified many times hence. An English Crusader Gilbert of Hastings was named its first bishop and the church was built on the site of the first Mosque of Lisbon.

King Dinis in the 13th century ordered a cloister to be built in the Gothic Style and it is in this place that we saw the Gothic Tomb of Knight Lopo Fernandes Pacheco, 7th Lord of Ferreira de Aves, in the ambulatory. His figure appears holding his sword and is guarded by a dog.

Since this is a 12th century church; it reminds from the outside of Notre Dame in Paris (from the pictures I have seen) and the "Igreja da Sé" in old Coimbra. It was a fortress church in its beginnings. It is the oldest church in Lisbon and is of Romanesque and Gothic design. It was huge and cavernous with just a few stained glass windows. There were Gothic niches with altars. Somewhere to the back of the main altar ("altar maior") there were the sarcophagi of an archbishop of the 14th century and the knight already mentioned. The building all seemed a bit dingy, but is impressive for its size and the entrance.

The Electric Trolley ["o Elétrico"] from the Alfama District

The Belvedere and the Electric Trolley Car, "O Elétrico," Lisbon

The first tramway in Lisbon entered service in 1873 as a horse car line, but all was converted to electricity in 1901. The Lisbon Metro and the bus system have of course reduced its use and importance. But it remains one of the few in Europe. Debate as to its usefulness continues in Lisbon. Our introduction to the tram was when we returned to the "Largo de São Miguel" and the "Chafariz de Baixo" looking down on the docks. Then we took a one and one half hour ride on the "elétrico," one of the electric street trollies still used all over Lisbon. The route started at the east side of the "Baixa" in the city center and did a complete circle coming out at the "Chiado" at Carmo. We were struck by the density of the city and its crowds, but also by its apparent poverty in what seemed not slums but grey, old, worn business districts. The passersby seemed drab with rather plain dress. There was intense traffic and a seeming total lack of parking space and greenness almost the entire route. It made Lisbon appear huge with cars parked everywhere including at the principal plaza the "Paço."

An aside: to this traveler the atmosphere seemed very different from the urban Brazil I knew of with its beaches and mountains. It lacked the relaxed atmosphere, the green of the tropics and bright clothes and music of Brazil. We actually found the trolley ride a bit depressing. Yet the massive and total poverty of the "favelas" of Brazil was not present. For me it recalled to mind the lower middle class sections of Guatemala City it the 1970s.

We stopped at Rossio Station which was jammed with huge crowds of commuters to the suburbs. This was the main railroad station of Lisbon of the Portuguese Royal Railway Company from 1886 to 1988, built on Rossio Square and connecting the city to Sintra. Service was restricted to a few long service lines in the early 1990s. It was built in the "Neo - Manueline" style typical of early 16th century Portugal. One notices the two intertwined horseshoe portals at the entrance. Inside there are ramps connecting to a cast-iron structure. Trains gain access to the station through a tunnel more than 2600 meters long.

I surmised it should be an easy ride to our destination of Sintra on another day.

Keah, Katie, Mark in the "Cervejaria" District, Lisbon

We enjoyed beers and talk at the bar district and ate the snails (caracóis) with the help of needles and then a delightful dinner at "Bom Jardim." We had "frango no espeto, salada de alface, tomate e cebola" accompanied by Matheus Rosé wine. There was cocoanut ice cream later and a taxi home. One sees throughout this book that I/we were not of gourmet persuasion. "Down home" Portuguese food, the closer to the Brazilian version the better, was our choice.

BELÉM

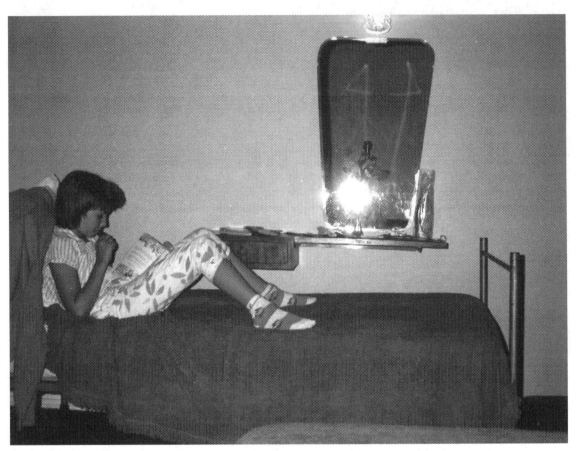

Katie and the "Plastic" Bed at the "Residência Dublin"

We dragged ourselves from bed at 8:20 after a very fitful night of sleep. The plastic bed coverings on Katie's bed and her tossing and turning might have had something to do with it. Not her fault! There was a light breakfast of "café com leite e pão." Katie was almost in hysterics (laughing) at what they called "orange juice," me too. It was a far cry from the freshly squeezed orange juice at the Hotel Tropical in Manaus or the Hotel da Bahia in Salvador.

We took a taxi to the "Cais de Sodré" train station; there was much less city traffic than at Rossio Station and it was a quick trip. The former station was in a poor area and reminded me of "Central do Brasil" in Rio. The commuter trains were electric, smooth and efficient. We traveled along the Rio Tejo for about fifteen minutes to Belém. Incidentally the ride cost 50 cents apiece.

Importance of Belém

Belém from the Portuguese word for "Bethlehem" is a civil parish in the municipalty of Lisbon. It is six kilometers west of city center and two kilometers west of the Bridge "Ponte 25 de Abril." The area became famous for its military position along the mouth of the Tagus, its role in the exploration of India and the Orient (the "Caminho das Indias") and then royal residences like the Palácio de Ajuda. It is famous for several monuments to be seen shortly.

Belém along the waterfront seemed old and a bit worse for wear, but up above the old part one could see there was a lot of new, shiny growth. It was evident that the middle and upper classes of greater Lisbon live outside the city center and the area of the trolley ride yesterday. Much of Belém seemed like Salvador's "orla" (the miles of beach and beach communities to the north of old Salvador) as compared to its old city. Cascais would confirm this view. The monuments follow.

Portuguese "Cafezinhos" or "Bicas" and Soda—a "Confeitaria" in Belém

Before tackling the monuments we had a nice "bica" and soft drink in a local café.

The Monastery of Belém ["O Mosteiro de Belém"]

The old hermitage on the spot was originally the home for the Hieronymite religious order <u>circa</u> 1459. It was originally administrated by monks of the religious-military Order of Christ. It was then enlarged and beautified into the great building it is today by King Manuel I and meant to be the resting place of the family members of the Casa dos Avis and as a church for seafaring adventurers who embarked during the Age of Discovery. In 1496 Manuel petitioned the Holy See to build the monastery at the entrance of Lisbon. Vasco da Gama and his men spent the night in prayer there at the older hermitage when departing for the Orient in 1497; upon his return in 1498 with samples of gold, it became a symbol and a house of prayer for seamen leaving the port.

Construction began again in 1501 and was completed 100 years later, the money coming from the five per cent tax on commerce from Africa and the Orient. Resources already planned for Batalha Monastery (to be seen later) were transferred here. Boitaca was the original architect, then a Spaniard, the style thus moving from Portuguese Manueline to Spanish Plateresque. All halted with King Manuel's death in 1521.

Manel I had ordered the Hieronymite monks occupying the monastery to pray for his eternal soul and spiritual assistance for navigators and sailors who departed from the Bay of Reselo to discover the world.

Felipe II of Spain in 1604 made the Monastery a royal funerary monument. It was restored to Portugal in 1640.

The tourist guides note and conflict with each other at times, saying that in 1682 in the reign of Pedro II of Portugal the bodies of King Sebastian and Cardinal Henrique were buried in the transept chapels. This presents an historical problem: most accounts of history say King Sebastian's body was never recovered after the tragic battle in Morocco in 1578. However, according to some sources, King Felipe II of Spain claimed to recover the remains of the body of Sebastian and had him buried in Jerônimos. But this is not proven and is debated.

Tomb of King Sebastião and the Elephants, "Mosteiro dos Jerônimos," Belém

At any rate, Sebastian's tomb is at least a "symbolic" tomb recalling one of the great stories of Portuguese culture and history. In 1578 young King Sebastian took on the formidable task of carrying the conquest of the Moors to their own lands in Morocco, but was soundly defeated and was killed at the battle of Alcácer Quibir. They never found the body and there were amazing consequences. A legend arose about the person never found and that young, reckless Sebastian would return one day and lead tiny Portugal to days of greater glory. It never happened, but the legend was transferred to the backlands of northeastern Brazil and produced more than one "messianic" figure claiming either to be or to be inspired by Sebastian to "save" Brazil. The "Pedra Bonita" massacre of the early eighteen hundreds (1829) and the more famous War of Canudos (1896-1897) with the Messianic leader Antônio Conselheiro are cases in point. The latter became the subject of what some say is the Brazilian National Epic, "Os Sertões" by the journalist-writer Euclides da Cunha. One noted that the tomb in Jerônimos was placed between marvelous carved elephants with tusks.

As a Brazilianist I have always had a problem with the exact literary role of "Os Sertões." First of all it is a work in prose, the result of the fieldnotes of the journalist Euclides da Cunha during the campaign of the war in 1896-1897. Does this qualify it as being an Epic? Certainly not in the traditional European sense of the word! Even then, many Braziians call it "Brazil's greatest novel." I protest even more strongly here. The book is written in prose and is based on Da Cunha's diary reworked into a sociological and journalistic account of the times. In no way is it fiction or can resemble a novel. Case closed. A great work and really important in the evolution of Brazilian literature, an Epic in the Euroopean sense (in verse and in ten "cantos) it is not. Perhaps I protest too much, but after all these years in the academy it was good to get it off my chest.

Tomb of Vasco da Gama, "Jerônimos"

There was much more to see in yet another chapel of the monastery of the "Jerônimos." In 1898, the 400th anniversary of the arrival of Vasco da Gama in India, they restored his tomb in "Jerônimos." One might recall that it was the Portuguese seafarers who first gained glory in the time of Christopher Columbus but prior to the later Spanish explorers one-half century later, a fact Portugal constantly reminds the world (and the Spanish).

The seafarer left Lisbon and Belem in 1497 and arrived on the coast of India in 1498, this after descending the west coast of Africa, rounding the cape of Good Hope, encountering Moslem pirates on the east coast of Africa (20th century pirates encountered recently already existed even then!) and braved fierce storms to finally arrive in Goa on the west coast of India. The villains however were made mythological and closely based on the gods and goddesses of the "Aeneid." Da Gama actually did a return trip four years later but it was the first that marked world history. No longer having to face the Moslem perils of the eastern Mediterranean or the Red Sea, Portugal opened up a true age of discovery in the Far East, including the Malaccas (near today's Indonesia and Malaysia,) the coast of China and eventually Japan. The treasures were the spices so highly valued in Europe at the time. And a related topic would be the adventures of the Jesuit Missionaries, among them Mateo Ricci and Francisco Xavier to China and Japan. Da Gama's great exploit would be the moving force and primary topic of the Portuguese national epic, "The Lusiads."

Tomb of Luís de Camões, "Jerônimos"

In the same chapel as Da Gama's tomb was the tomb of one of his greatest admirers, Luís de Camões, Portugal's most famous writer who wrote the Portuguese epic poem "The Lusiads" [Os Lusíadas"] in the early 16th century. Camões was one of the reasons I wanted to see Portugal. I had a wonderful reading of the poem in graduate school at Saint Louis University under the tutelage of Dr. Doris Turner who also introduced us to the highlights of Brazilian Literature. And much later in my time as faculty at ASU I actually had the opportunity to teach the master work in a graduate reading course.

The poem is a true epic poem in octaves and tells the tale of the great Portuguese voyages of discovery to the Far East in the 15th century. It is a Renaissance version of the epic verse form and Camões had no qualms about basing much of its style on Virgil's "Aeneid" which of course in turn borrowed heavily from the "Iliad" and "Odyssey" of Homer and the Greek epic tradition. The poem in ten "cantos" placed tiny Portugal on the literary map of Europe. One also notes that Camões and this epic poem are the trademarks of Portuguese high culture in the academy. In fact the Portuguese language came to be called "the Language of Camões." I came to realize the significance of all this in 1973 in Rio de Janeiro in the "Gabinete Real de Leitura Portuguesa," one of the great cultural spots in Brazil, where the great scholars of the times on Portuguese Literature, the "Lusiads" and Camões, all waxed eloquent in praise of the same. It was a real lesson in Portuguese tradition. I was amazed then and am still amazed at the importance of the author and his works in Portugal.

Camões' life is an epic as well. I think there are real parallels with Cervantes in Spain. With privileged parents he was able to study with the Dominicans and the Jesuits, and although perhaps not enrolled, spent significant time at the University of Coimbra. He lost an eye after serving as a soldier at the Battle of Ceuta in Africa in the 1500s. But what most changed him was the military and bureaucratic service in long years in the Far East, eventually as a burocrat in Macau with the unpleasant task of dealing with recovery of goods of the deceased Portuguese and their return to Portugal. He was not impressed by the level of honesty in general in such days. He was involved in shipwrecks, battles with Muslims, pirates and the like. After writing his masterpiece during this time in the far East based on the Vasco da Gama voyage (one legend is that he almost lost it in a shipwreck near the Mekong Delta and actually swam to shore with it in his hand!), and returning home to Portugal and short-lived literary fame, he experienced the low point of Portuguese history of the times, the news of the loss by Portugal to the Moors in 1578 in the Battle of Alcácer Quibir (today's Morocco) and the death of the young King Sebastião. Worse was that this left the Portuguese throne open to Spain's Felipe II by virtue of royal marriage and blood lines. Portugal had long ago (in 1385) battled to be independent from Spain and this brought a new nightmare to patriots, among the greatest Camões himself. He in fact died at the beginning of the Spanish domination in 1580.

Yours truly knelt before both tombs of Vasco da Gama and Camões in homage to these great men studied in the graduate courses at Saint Louis University years ago. Not being so sure about King Sebastian's, I just marveled at the elephants with tusks in front of the marble "edifice."

Cloister, Katie and Fountain, "Jerônimos"

Katie, Lion and Fountain, "Jerônimos"

The cloister and fountains were equally impressive, all in the Manueline style. The style was actually given its name by Count Varnhagen in 1842 when writing about the style of the "Mosteiro de Belém." It refers to the king of the time when the architectue was so used, King Manuel I ("Casa dos Avis"). The style is linked to "Jerônimos" and influence from the time of Portuguese discoveries from Africa to the Far East. Short-lived from 1490 to 1520, it was seen in churches, monasteries, palaces and castles. Some say it combines late Gothic with Spanish Plateresque, "Mudéjar," and Italian and Flemish architecture. Themes are from the people, fauna and flora of the voyages of discovery and the Far East.

The Tower of Belém ["A Torre de Belém"]

"A Torre de Belém"

It was constructed by King João II as part of a defensive system to protect access to the Tagus estuary. Originally called the "Tower of São Vicente," it was finished by Manuel I of Portugal (1515-1520) to guard the entrance to the port at Belém. And of course the architecture is "Manuelina." It is interesting to know that the Portuguese accompanied the construction of the actual tower with a "second team," a huge ship anchored nearby to defend the entrance to Lisbon, the "Grande Nau" of 1100 tons. Over the succeeding years the Tower was used as fortress, dungeon, custom house, and even light house.

This is a fortress on the Rio Tejo dating from the same period as the Monastery. It was from this point that the caravels left for Africa, Asia and America. It was very interesting with a stone block tower, winding stairway and turrets, a beautiful setting by the river.

A minor curious tourist aside: there was a ventriloquist on the train from Lisbon to Belém. Katie was impressed! She was a good sport and traveling companion. Shortly after we arrived in Belém and before the monuments we had "bicas" and soft drinks in a delightful café facing the waterfront, and of course Katie's now favorite "croks."

The Monument to the Discoverers ["Monumento dos Descobridores"]

"Monumento dos Descobridores"—Monument of the Discoverers, Belém

This is a fifty-two meter high slab of concrete, erected in 1960 to commemorate the 500th anniversary of the death of Prince Henry the Navigator (we shall talk of him later). One may recall that it was Portugal in the 15th century that developed many of the mainstays of ocean travel in those unchartered times, among them the invention of the "Caravel" ship and sails which allowed tacking into the wind. It was on such ships with the help of the astrolabe for sighting stars that Portugal came to dominate the seven seas. Prince Henry was behind much of it.

Side view of the Monument of the Discoverers

It was sculpted in the form of a caravel ship's prow with dozens of figures from Portuguese history ascending to a statue of the "Infante" Henry the Navigator, all sculpted in base relief. Adjacent to the monument is a "calçada" or square in the form of a map, showing the routes of various Portuguese explorers from the Age of Discovery.

The "Museu dos Coches"

The Royal Carriage Museum, "O Museu dos Coches," Belém

The nobility had to get around in those days, and this museum has many fine examples of the old "diligencias" or "stagecoaches." It is interesting to know that the museum is housed in the old horse riding arena of the Belém Palace, now the official residence of the President of Portugal. The Museum was begun by Queen Amélia in 1905 and has samples from the 16th to the 19th centuries, among them the traveling coach of King Philip II of Portugal (Felipe II of Spain) used for travel from Spain to Portugal in 1619. Several of the coaches are related to the Vatican, either donated to the Portuguese Crown or used by the Portuguese Ambassador to the Vatican in the 18th century.

Mark and Keah at the "Bom Jardim"

After that long day of seeing the best of Belém's monuments, supper once again was at the "Bom Jardim" with "frango no espeto." We were super tired at that point and rather miserable. It was a great sightseeing day however.

May 31ˢᵗ.

It seemed to be the world's worst night of sleep so we slept in and got up late, feeling horrible but coffee helped a bit. We attended mass in a modern concrete church and I understood just a word or two of the service, a victim once again of a really poor sound system, lousy acoustics, and I suspect, some colloquial Portuguese. We walked to the Marquês de Pombal statue by the Residência Nazareth and had a lunch of "pregos, mixtos, e sorvete." The mid-day meal would change and improve greatly and conform to "normal" Portuguese custom on our future forays outside Lisbon, but the evening repast at the "Bom Jardim" never failed to please and really took its place for us. I guess we were still used to the U.S. lunch fare.

There was a short visit to the Gulbenkian Museum where we saw many paintings by Rubens, Degas, Monet, Manet, Turner and Renois. Keah is the in - house expert on modern French Art.

We walked down a very pretty long park and checked out the Ritz and Meridian Hotels where "the other side" was living. Our day would come but not yet.

Then there was a taxi to the "Bom Jardim" with beers in the "beco das cervejarias" and the now usual dinner. We loved it, why change? We dined on "frango no espeto, batata frita, salada de cebola e tomate, flan e Mateus Rosé."

June 1st.

Katie Wading in the Surf, Cascais

After a good night's sleep we went to a travel agency to arrange travel outside Lisbon along with the requisite hotel reservations. Then we took a bus and the train to Cascais and the beaches, farther west on the coast from Belém.

The town was originally connected to administration by Sintra, but became an important fishing village and supplier for Lisbon in the 13th and 14th centuries. One of the most interesting facets of its history was during World War II when it became the home of many of the exiled royal families of Europe fleeing from the Fascist threat of World War II. Portugal remained neutral in it all, an amazing turn of events. It was a modern tourst town, complete with casino, "plaza de toros," and such for the modern tourists.

There was an ill-fated taxi trip to "Boca do Inferno" (the driver with impossible to understand Portuguese), supposedly the westernmost point of Portugal with a high peak overlooking the cold Atlantic. The view was great; it was the difficulty of communication in the taxi that was difficult. We then came back to Cascais to the Café Bristol for lunch. The sea, the fishing boats, and beach at Cascais were pretty. It seemed to be a nice resort atmosphere for the upper class. Katie waded a bit in the sea.

SINTRA

An Historic Overview

The Moorish fort may have existed since the 8th or 9th century A.D. Earliest times show it as a Moorish establishment with fort, this as early as the 11th century. The ubiquitous Afonso Henriques captured Sintra in 1147 after the fall of Lisbon.

One story has it that Christopher Columbus, now sailing for the Spanish Crown, was blown off course in 1493, spotted the rock of Sintra and sailed safely into Lisbon harbor.

The architect of Batalha, Boitac, built the Hieronymite monastery of "Nossa Senhora da Pena" in 1507. The building would evolve into the "Palácio da Pena." It would become the summer palace of the Braganças in the 18th and 19th centuries.

This is a Michelin Three Star Attraction and it lived up to that rating. The tourists were up at 7:30, had the "pequeno almoço" at 8:00 and were to Rossio Station at 9:00. The train to Sintra left at 9:08!

As we left, the station was jammed with many trains and all the commuter traffic. The scenery to Sintra was null and void until we reached the outskirts of Sintra on a trip of 18 miles and in 45 minutes by the "comboio," the strange name Portugal has for such trains.

View into Sintra—the "Palácio da Pena"

All of a sudden there is a huge castle high on a hill to the left. Spectacular! There are three palaces in town: the 16th century Royal Palace in the town center, the Moorish Castle on the hill and the Bragança palace the "Palácio da Pena" way up on the mountain, the most recent.

Katie and Keah, "O Palácio Real," Sintra

It is the best preserved medieval palace in Portugal, lived in continuously from the 15th to the late 19th century. After two hundred years the place was really added to and remodeled by King Manuel. The result is that one half of the Royal Palace is Manuelino Style, and there is more recent architecture in the other. The inside was full of the famous blue Portuguese tiles ("azulejos") but made for Manuel in Sevilla in Spain. The guide noted that furnishings were Spanish, Moroccan, East Indian, and Brazilian. The tour included the huge bakery with its large chimney. One room with its painted ceiling had a theme of "magpies," another with swans ("cisnes"), a painting of the twenty-seven year old daughter of King Dom Diniz and Spanish wife Isabella, the Coat of Arms of the Avis Dynasty and its descendants, and the tale of a prince held prisoner (he was "louco") for nine years. Shades of Prince Segismundo in the Spaniard Golden Age Playwright Calderón de la Barca's famous "La Vida Es Sueño"! The Bragança nobility, in particular Queen Amélia, liked the place and still used it as a part time residence in the 19th century. It became a national monument in 1940.

The Main Plaza of Sintra and the Moorish Castle Above

I wrote that the town center seemed like "Fantasyland" in Disneyland in Los Angeles, perhaps with good reason—Disney did research and copied palaces and castles at his place of business. The Spaniards, however, say the big palace in Segovia is the model for the castle of "Fantasyland." There were palaces with turrets and parapets all about.

The "Palácio da Pena"

Entrance, "Palácio da Pena"

We took a taxi up the steep hill to the "Palácio da Pena" or "Cliff Palace." It is considered one of the major sites of 19th Century Romanticism in the world! I believe it; the heart not the mind inspired this place! They describe it as Neo-Gothic, Neo-Manueline, Neo-Islamic and Neo-Renaissance. It's all there. It became a summer residence for the Braganças and is still used on special occasions by the head of state of Portugal. Not to be missed! It dates to the 14th century but it was King Manuel I (Avis) who ordered a monastery built on the site with, who else, the "Jerônimos" in charge. The earthquake of 1755 reduced most of it to ruins but King Ferdinand and Queen Maria II had it rebuilt in the mid 19th century. Several different architects of divese nationalities participated. One note is that one of them specialized in castles along the Rhine and brought a splash of those fairy tale castles to "Pena."

One might recall that the same royal family the Braganças fled to Rio de Janeiro during Napoleon's invasion of Portugal around 1803 and only returned in 1814—minus son Pedro who would become Emperor of Brazil with his "I'm staying"["Eu fico"] speech from the "Palácio do Paço" in "Praça 15" in Rio de Janeiro. The palace in one sense was almost a bit humorous—such a hodgepodge of styles! It appeared to be the result of a drunken party by a half dozen architects gathered together to outdo each other!

West Parapet, "Palácio da Pena"

Northwest Parapet, "Palácio da Pena"

Interior Pátio with "Azulejos," "Palácio da Pena"

One recalls all the blue tiles, stone lattice work, gargoyles of crocodiles, but most impressive were the high parapets with the view toward Lisbon and the Rio Tejo to one side, to Cascais to the west, and up north along the Atlantic Coast. It was said that the Duke of Wellington spied Napoleon's troops from the NW parapet and soon the battle to retake the peninsula ensued.

It was a truly spectacular view. There was a fierce wind from the ocean side. One recalls the interior rooms with "gesso" or plaster decoration in the Arabic "mudéjar" style and also much marble and wood. There were many tapestries, Persian and the like, many chandeliers and candelabras. But it still seemed a bit old and dingy, a bit freaky. It was difficult to imagine the steep ride up the mountain by horse drawn carriage!

View Down to the "Castelo Mouro" from the "Palácio da Pena"

There is an amazing history to the castle: after the loss of Córdoba in Spain to the Almorávides dynasty in 1031, the King of Badajoz opted to transfer to Alfonso VI of León and Castile some territories on the Iberian Peninsula, among them the castle at Sintra. Afonso Henriques in 1147 with the capture of Lisbon took control of this place as well.

From the parapets of the Palácio da Pena one actually looks DOWN on the "Castelo Mouro." One can imagine the Moorish defense of the area from the high parapets and what the Portuguese must have had to do to take the old Moorish Castle and then keep it from the Spaniards and later the French. From the Moorish Castle there are views up to the "Palácio da Pena" and down to the main plaza in town. We decided to walk down; it was a long, long hike down the trail but through great forest! The latter was carefully planned and has trees from throughout the world.

"Louça" and Shops

Portuguese China or "Louça," Sintra

There was time for sightseeing in the main plaza where we saw the outstanding examples of Portuguese ceramic pottery. We spent a good part of that day with Jack and Kathleen, tourists from London who were good company. Katie loved them and babbled to anyone knowing English!

In sum, the ole' professor admits he was scared to death of the heights and narrow walkways around the parapets of the "Palácio da Pena" and then the walls of the Moorish castle. But this is what Portugal and Spain are all about! I never saw a castle wall or walkway that I did not want to climb! I will speak much of this later, including the cliché of "castles in Spain," but suffice to say Portugal indeed has its share, and in one sense is just a "small Spain.

A Belated Cultural Note on Sintra:

Portugal's classic poet Gil Vicente, its epic poet Camões and England's Lord Byron have all sung Sintra's praise (the latter in "Childe Harold"). To summarize the area: the Moorish castle dates from the 8th century and includes ruins of a Romanesque chapel. The big palace of the town center was built in the 14th century with wings added on by King Manuel in the 16th. The Palácio da Pena was rebuilt in the 19th century by Fernando II, a Bragança, but includes ruins of an old Manueline chapel and cloister from the 16th century with its Portuguese tiles and Carrera marble altar.

Sintra was the summer residence of Portuguese royalty for six centuries. The Duke of Wellington signed the peace treaty with Napoleon at this site in 1814.

Exhausted from the day, we took the "local" train back to Lisbon, stopped by the tourist agency once again and then to the "Bom Jardim."

June 3

We got up late after the best night's sleep yet in Portugal. We hustled to the tourist agency to talk to Senhor Grilo (I don't know if this is ironic; "João Grilo" in Brazil is a great trickster!) who arranged for the trip north via telex and phone, arranging for all reservations and bus tickets. Grilo also arranged the ticket to Málaga coming up in a few days.

A small but important moment: we went to the "Texas Lavamática" on Bernadino Ribeiro Street and had great laundry service for 800 escudos. U.S. style laundromats during this time were a rarity in both Portugal and Spain.

"Elevador Santa Justa," Lisbon

We paid the bill at the less than desirable Residência Dublin and returned to the travel agency where they told us all was just perfect - "perfeito, perfeito!" Then there was a walk to Rossio Plaza, a later look at the Elevador Santa Justa (built of steel and "imitating" the Eiffel Tower) for three miserably tired tourists, and a perfect sunset outside the "Castelo de São Jorge" looking over the "Rio Tejo" once again. Then we trekked off for a final night in Lisbon at the "Bom Jardim" and packing for the big departure or "saída" to the North.

June 4

After a terrible night's sleep and revived just a bit with the coffee, we took a taxi to the "Rodoviária Nacional" and got on our first inter-city bus for a ride to nearby Alcobaça. It was good to be in the country; there were vineyards all along the way, some fields of wheat or barley, lots of olive trees and orange as well. The towns along the road seemed small and poor, but once again the peasants did not look as poor as those in the old North East in Brazil. The "Rio Tejo" was on the right for part of the journey. We had passed modern "Cidade Universitária" in Lisbon on the way out of town. There were pine forests, eucalyptus groves and always—vineyards.

Windmill or "Moinho de Vento" on the Road to Alcobaça

Shortly before Alcobaça there was a beautiful scene—windmills ["moinhos de vento"] in the pretty, green hills. Of course Spanish majors could only think of Don Quixote!

ALCOBAÇA

Entrance, "O Mosteiro de Alcobaça"

Blue Tiles, the Scene of Afonso Henriques' Plea to the Virgin

It was founded by no less than Afonso Henriques in approximately 1153 to pay a promise to the Blessed Virgin for her help in his victory over the Moors at nearby Santarém marking one of the high points of the Portuguese "Reconquista." The plan was to consolidate the young king's authority in the area and promote colonization to the area. The ticket would be the Cistercians under Bernard of Clairvaux who would build a major medieval monastery. It was huge by any measure with a 350 foot long nave, 70 foot high Gothic vault, Gothic front door and windows. There were many additions in the 16th century. It is indeed one of the major monasteries of all Europe!

Sarcophagus of Inés de Castro

Once again Portuguese Literature enters our story. Famous in Portuguese History and Letters were King Pedro and his lover Inés de Castro, his Spanish lady-in-waiting. Their love affair told in a romantic legend known to all is still required reading in Portuguese grammar schools. Alcobaça Monastery held their tombs which are considered the best examples of sculpture of the 14th century in Portugal. Inés was disliked by Pedro's father Afonso IV who feared Castilian influence in Portugal; he ordered Inés' death by decapitation. Upon learning of this Pedro who truly loved her and claimed she was the lawful queen and inheritor had her killers murdered, their hearts ripped out "because they had none" and then according to legend commanded all in the Portuguese court to pay homage to her by kissing the rotting bones of the hand of the corpse! The sarcophagi in Alcobaça depict Pedro and Inés both rising to look at each other before entering eternity. The sides of the same sculpted tombs depict the hell reserved for their enemies.

Other highlights in the monastery were the huge cloister built and inspired by Dom Dinis in the 15th century, the dining hall and kitchen with a small stream channeled through, the sleeping quarters and finally the Room of the Kings, "Salão dos Réis." The latter had "azulejos" on all sides depicting the history of the founding of the Monastery, in particular Afonso Henriques on his knees praying for the intercession of the Virgin against the vile Moors at the Battle of Santarem. That latter tiled scene is located at the top of this segment.

View of Alcobaça Monastery from Hotel, Katie, Keah

Tourism and Our Hotel the Santa Maria

Our hotel in Alcobaça was a pleasant change from the "Residência Dublin" with the former's fourth floor room with a veranda overlooking the historically famous huge monastery and main plaza of Alcobaça. Before seeing the monastery we had visited shops with the famous Portuguese "louça" or ceramic china and scenes of blue tile. In one shop Mark bought his "Portuguese fishing cap" or "boné de linho" and got information for our next destination, the town and beach of Nazaré and the Porto de Abrigo.

We had a dinner of "vitela, batata frita, arroz, ervilhas, cenoura, pão e manteiga e morangos." It was accompanied by "vinho branco." It was delicious, and incidentally, I noted that the total bill was $14 U.S. The next morning we enjoyed breakfast overlooking the Monastery. Katie had enjoyed "Alf" on TV the night before in English! There was a bit of frustration changing travelers' checks with the usual bank bureaucracy. All was followed by a quick taxi to the bus station and a "milk run" of thirty miles, 30 cents U.S. for each of us, through Valado followed by a train hookup and suddenly we were in Nazaré on the Atlantic Ocean. There were flowers, vineyards and hills along the way.

NAZARÉ

View of Nazaré

It was all they promised it would be—a fisherman's town along the sea, the town made a national monument. There was a small, quality beach in a crescent with wonderful waves, the ocean a turquoise-blue in the sunshine. There are high cliffs to one side (the highest in Portugal along the Atlantic Coast) and a funicular up the mountain to the "Nossa Senhora do Nazaré" shrine and church. Vasco da Gama was here before and after the India trip! One can see why it is a favorite tourist spot for the English as well as others from Northern Europe, especially during the hot days of August when the tiny place is transformed. In late May we had it to ourselves; in August the entire beach is crammed with beach tents and umbrellas.

View of Funicular to Top of Nazaré Hill

From the top of the hill there was a magnificent view of the town below and out to sea. On this hill is the church of "Nossa Senhora do Nazaré" which owes its existence to the legend of Dom Fuas Roupinho from 1182. Hunting with friends, he was in hot pursuit of a deer and arrived at the precipice overlooking the ocean in the midst of heavy fog. Suddenly realizing he would go over the edge he appealed to the Virgin asking her aid; she responded and he and his horse were saved in mid air. The chapel of the Virgin remains on the cliff edge. Of importance is the fact that the huge cult of the "Virgem do Nazaré" in Belém do Pará in Brazil is based upon the same memory of the Virgin. The feast days in Brazil last for an entire month! Yours truly was able to return to Belém and the Basílica de Nazaré in very recent days; the festivities and religious fervor are a sight to behold!

Church in Nazaré with Blue Tile Façade

    One of the churches in town displayed exterior walls entirely of azulejos and beautiful images and flowers within. This church is linked to the Portuguese fishermen and families. They fished the outer banks, caught millions of cod and many immigrated to Portuguese New England in places like New Bedford, MA. There they are associated with the huge whaling industry; many of the residents migrated not from the mainland but from the Azores which were already involved with the harvesting of whales in the Atlantic.

Fishermen's Wives Sewing on the Beach

The best word for the town is "quaint." The narrow streets of the town were of cobblestone, and we saw laundry on the balconies of the white washed houses and there were flowers about. It was a truly pretty scene. We had a large meal at the Ribamar Restaurant: "sopa de mar," a shrimp omelet, and "robalo" or sea bass. Then walking out to the beach we saw this scene: the women, fishermen's wives, are picturesque; during the day they sit in the sand mending nets while wearing black shawls and a short skirt with many petticoats. I wondered if the local tourist commission paid them to be in such a prominent place.

Fishermen Mending Nets at Dusk on the Beach

The men are in plaid shirts with long black stocking caps. In the late afternoon, between about 5 and 7 p.m. the men are also lying on the beach talking, the women knitting. A few tourists are along the "passeio" gawking at this "folkloric" sight. At least part of the daily catch was displayed on drying racks on the beach during the sunny part of the day.

Drying Fish ("Carrapú") on Racks on Nazaré Beach

Katie, Keah with Young Girls on Fishing Boat at Nazaré

One of the last scenes on that beautiful day, along with the fish racks, the ladies knitting on the beach, and the men mending nets, was the felicitous moment of spying one of the old style traditional fishing boats. Some tourists and locals mingled to enjoy it all.

Katie Wading in the Surf at Nazaré

I forgot to mention that earlier in the day Katie waded along the entire beach and we all watched while the small fishing boats came in.

A tourist aside: Portugal is a principal site for tourists from England and we met several of them in our journey to the north. We were in Nazaré well before high season, but in the European months of vacation of July and August the village is jammed with tourists. The weather is then much warmer and all love the beach. One tourist would tell us of the British tourist route: the Chunnel across the sea from England to the coast of France and the "freeway" directly down the coast to Spain and Santander and west toward Spain's Santiago de Compostela and then down to Portugal. It is to be noted that the principal market for Portugal's wines including its famous "Port" is indeed England.

On June 6 we left delightful Nazaré with its beach, ocean and fishermen by local bus ("expresso" means they stop only at the bus stations) to the next destination of Óbidos. It took about one hour, staying close to the coast, driving by São Martinho and its bay on the left, and then through hills inland.

ÓBIDOS

Overview of Walls and Castle of Óbidos

The town is small and quaint, a medieval town within a wall. Inside the walled city is a castle at one end which today has been converted into a "Pousada" built into the wall. The original castle and wall were built by the Moors and had been used to fortify the coastal route. They were rebuilt by the Portuguese after the town was freed by Afonso Henriques in 1048. King Dom Dinis and his queen visited in 1228. She was taken with the place so he gave the town to her as a gift! The tradition of the Portuguese king giving the town to his queen continued until 1833. More incidental historical notes: in 1491 King João II (Avis dynasty) died in Santarém and his body was found in the "Rio Tejo." His wife Queen Leonor went to Óbidos to mourn. Much later The Duke of Wellington spied the French army from Óbidos in 1808 and thus began the first battle of the campaign to retake the peninsula.

Another View of Walls and Castle of Óbidos

As mentioned, the ramparts of the walls of Óbidos date from Moorish occupation but were restored in the 12th, 13th, and 16th centuries. The Castle Keep is on the north, the setting of today's "Pousada."

Katie and Armored Knight in the Castle of Óbidos

In the visit to the "Pousada" Katie preened beside a complete suit of Portuguese armor! We walked as much of the walls as possible with a wonderful view and a sense of history!

Mark and the Church of Óbidos

The inside walls of St. Mary's Church were entirely of "azulejos"! King Alfonso V married his eight year old cousin Isabella here in 1444. The rest of the town is quaint with pretty stucco houses, many flowers, cobblestones, tile roofs and azulejos. It really is a small place, quite compact.

Ice Cream—Óbidos

We enjoyed ice cream in Óbidos and then meeting English tourists. There was dinner at Josefa D'Óbidos' restaurant, eating with Alec from London who was "motoring" through Portugal and Spain. He was humorous and a bit superior in his attitude toward Portugal and the Portuguese. The Currans were exhausted by the tourism of the day and were soon to bed.

June 7 and Travel

We were up early at 6 a.m., contracted a sleepy taxi driver to Caldas, and then were back on the bus which retraced our route to Nazaré which was clouded in today. Then we took a cobblestone road to Leiria. Along the route there were pine forests, sawmills and furniture factories. We saw the main plaza and castle from the distance. This bus is the "milk run" to Batalha and stops at each "paragem." There were peasants on the bus to Batalha and I understood zero of their Portuguese.

BATALHA

A Stylish Katie on the Diving Board at the Motel in Batalha

After the arrival in Batalha we then took a taxi just one kilometer to the small hotel, more like a country bungalow with a pool. And then we enjoyed a very welcomed "café com leite e páo."

Batalha, its history and a high point of Portuguese-Spanish history—Aljubarrota, 1385

Juan I of Castile, nephew of the deceased Portuguese king, and João I, Grand Master of the Order of Avis (crowned king in Portugal just seven days earlier) meet in battle to decide the crown of Portugal. João makes a promise to the Virgin to build a church in her honor should he win. He takes the day when his general Nuno Álvares Pereira chases the Spanish all the way back to Castile. The result was the great Gothic church "Santa Maria da Vitória da Batalha." And Portugal becomes free of Spanish domination for 200 years.

O Mosteiro da Batalha

The "Façada" of the "Mosteiro da Batalha"

A Lateral View of the "Mosteiro" and General Nunes de Pereira

The real name of the sublime edifice is the "Mosteiro de Maria Vitoriosa da Batalha" and was begun in 1388 by a Portuguese architect. Then construction continued in 1402 to 1438 by Houget, an Irish architect who did the Gothic "Founder's Chapel" in "flamboyant Gothic."

The Royal Sarcophagus, Batalha

King João I (Avis), spouse Philippa of Lancaster and son Prince Henry the Navigator are buried here. We digress to tell of this famous son. The great Portuguese Age of Discovery all started with the impetus of "Henrique o Navegador." He had encouraged his father to invade Ceuta in Northern Africa and also got everyone interested in the legend of Christian Prester John. Defeating the Moors in Ceuta also temporarily solved the problem of the Barbary pirates who had invaded the coast of Portugal and hauled off victims to the African slave market. It was Henry who was instrumental in the Portuguese development of the "Caravela" or lighter sailing ship that could tack into the wind; these were the ships that would soon conquer the sea lanes, to the east to India, to the West to Brazil. Henry was incidentally governor of the Order of Christ, the Portuguese version of the Knights of Templar in the city of Tomar. The Templar funds aided him in obtaining the goods and the ships to carry out his goals. His place of work was Sagres in the Algarve where he gathered map makers and navigators. It is said that the greatest secrets of the ages were indeed the maps! All led to the discovery of the Azores and to the famous later expeditions of Bartolomeu Dias (the Cape of Good Hope) and Vasco da Gama's epic journey to India.

The main cloister of Batalha Monastery was done by Portuguese architect F. D'Évora who also did the Alfonso V Cloister in Gothic style. However, successor architects like Boiytac used the Manueline style in the arches of the cloister and in the Octagonal Royal Chapel (it was to be King Duarte's tomb). All work was abandoned by King João III (1521-1557) who favored doing a NEW monastery by the Hieronymites in Belém, the same one we described in previous pages. The Dominicans would administrate old Batalha.

Miscellaneous points of interest at the Batalha Monastery

The stained glass above the main altar is 16th century Manueline style.

The Fleur-de-Lis balustrade on the entire cloister combines Gothic and Manueline. There are flowered pinnacles, and slender columns with decorations of coils, pearls and shells.

The vaulting of the Chapel House is square, twenty by sixty feet, without supporting columns. The window is 16th century.

One enters the unfinished chapels via a Gothic Porch with the doorway in Manueline style of 16th century.

Added to the Octagonal Chapel is a Renaissance Balcony done by King João III in 1533.

The Cloister, Batalha

The important characteristic of the Gothic - the flying buttresses support the main walls allowing them to be thicker with larger vaults.

Main Door of Batalha Monastery

The huge doorway is entirely carved in stone with Christ in Majesty in the center, the four evangelists in the tympanum, the twelve apostles to the side and angels, prophets, kings and saints in the arching.

"Bicas" in the "Confeitaria," Batalha

After spending most of the day seeing the ins and outs of the Monastery, we had a 3 p.m. lunch including "Vinho Verde" and a taste of "Porto" in an incredibly busy, middle-upper class "confeitaria" or tea room located in a shopping area in Batalha. There were ladies dressed in high heels and their Sunday best, children nicely dressed, men in coat and tie, all gulping down "bicas," huge pastries, "sandes" or dainty sandwiches, and drinks. It was a very polite Sunday afternoon outing! We sat back, relaxed and enjoyed it. Katie reads constantly, keeping very busy. This was perhaps our only encounter with a "dressed up" Portugal.

Vignettes of the rest of that day at "Batalha:"

Keah is taking a picture from a parking spot in front of the tea shop and a dwarf steps in to park a car behind her.

A little boy sees pastries in the glass window of the "confeitaria" and licks the glass case in front.

Now there is heavy rain and we enjoy a nice dinner at our lodging the Motel São Jorge: "corvina, bife, salada, batata cozida, flan e vinho Matheus". There were roses at the table, and more importantly, the heater was on in the room. There were roses and all sorts of flowers in the garden. In the motel São Jorge at Batalha there was a TV interlude with funny British TV comedies with no dialogue (Mr. Bean), thus meant for an international audience. We all howled; the humor was very British or Continental.

It was very cool with a cold wind the next morning. We took a taxi to a small taxi stop in Batalha and went to a busy working people's café. We saw a lady with eggs heading to the market and "pedreiros" working on a new sidewalk. Men in the café were talking of the 2-1 win by Benfica over Sporting in a soccer match. There had been large buses with flags waving zooming by heading to Lisbon and the game.

I add a note from the travel diary as to the countryside we saw around Batalha.

There were tiny plots of great variety—wheat, vegetables, many fruit orchards and mostly vineyards with what looked like a plentiful harvest of grapes on them. The roads were winding between the hills and were badly paved. People seemed to board or get off the bus at every turn of the road. The countryside seems densely populated. There were some "burros," a few oxen and many small garden tractors pulling small wagons also used as transportation on the country highways. The farmers do not appear lower class or poor, and there is a very Celtic-Irish look to many. Traffic was often clogged but there were no real traffic jams. Our buses were great; from our seats with large windows we could see all the scenery. And the drivers were not scary like in Latin America. All this was the scene on our way to Fátima twenty-five minutes from Batalha. The ride was pleasant and the station was near the town.

As I rewrite these old notes I realize how small Portugal is but also how we really got a feeling for the countryside and the small towns north or Lisbon.

FÁTIMA

On the 13th of each month, especially in May and October, huge crowds of pilgrims come to Fátima to remember the dates of the first and then the final apparitions of the Virgin Mary to the peasant children. On May 13, 1917, the Virgin appeared from an oak tree to three shepherds, Francisco, Jacinta and Lúcia, and her message was a call for peace (it is 1917 and World War I still rages) and the conversion of Russia. On October 13, 1917, seventy thousand people were present and saw the rain stop and the sun shine and begin to revolve in the sky like a ball of fire. The Bishop of Leiria authorized the belief in the apparitions in 1930.

It was a pleasant ride over from the Batalha area; we had a great "breakfast" at a bakery—the main item almost an entire "pão de ló" or Angel Food Cake.

The Basílica of Fátima

We walked to the huge square of Fátima, impressive for its size.

The Chapel, Mass and Image of the Virgin, Fátima

The modern chapel where the tiny original chapel was built has columns with statues which represent the place and figures of the original apparitions. There was a wonderful mass in English, the high point being the singing in Latin, including the "Pater Noster." It took me back to the days of my youth - "Introibo ad altare dei" - or something like that. I prayed for and offered the mass to my Mom, a life time devotee of Fátima. She said her Rosary religiously every night. I recall in the winter time her being wrapped in her robe in front of the small heat register in the dining room of the old farm house with her beads in her hands. She was a great believer in the messages of Fátima, particularly praying for the conversion of Russia! I was very much moved by these brief moments in Fátima, far more than in Lourdes later in the summer.

The Basilica itself is modern with stained glass windows depicting the apparition scenes. It houses the tombs of the three shepherds. They told us that just a few days earlier the huge plaza was jammed with pilgrims, numbering perhaps in the hundreds of thousands. It was practically empty when we visited that morning.

LEIRIA

After Fátima the bus went through a mountainous region, low mountains to be sure, and many small villages. On the ride to Leiria in the fields every inch seemed to be planted and utilized. We saw "viñas" or vineyards, corn, wheat, orchards, and vegetable gardens.

An aside: Portuguese India and Africa. In Nazaré we encountered a fellow from Goa who badmouthed the Portuguese in his country of India. And there was a fellow from Angola with the opposite opinion, speaking in favor of the Dutch and Portuguese colonization in Africa. He said the Cubans troops "assisting Angola to ward off colonial power" in the 1980s robbed Luanda blind after the war taking cars and any mechanical devices or appliances off to Cuba. The blacks in Angola were considered menial laborers ["mão de obra"] by the Cubans and were unprepared to govern themselves. According to him Angola is a mess in spite of the fact it has minerals and good agricultural resources.

Leiria in the Beiras was a pleasant city along the Lis River. We stayed at the very pleasant "Pensão Ramalhete" for $28 a night, the best "buy" on the trip. It was clean, freshly painted, and all the plumbing worked well. There was a quaint "antique" bar, sitting room and dining room with a good breakfast of "presunto, chorizo, galletas, pão, manteiga, marmelada, e café com leite".

The Castle of Leiria from the Plaza

We walked to a nice local park and watched local ladies having their "bicas," then walked along the river and up to the castle high on the hill. We heard an interesting version of local history by the guide who spoke beautiful, clearly pronounced, professional Portuguese (a rarity on the trip by the guides) and lectured us on Leiria's role in Portuguese history, all a bit amplified I think.

After the "lecture" there were still questions in my mind. Did the Moors ever actually have a castle here? Was it their defensive redoubt while taking the Peninsula? It turns out that Afonso Henriques won the area in the 12th century but it was retaken twice by the Moors. Leiria and the castle were later occupied by King Dom Dinis and Queen Isabella in the 14th century; she later became a saint by the Catholic Church. Locals say it was from here that Dom Dinis founded the University of Coimbra.

From the balcony within the walls of the castle there was a beautiful view of the town. The old Gothic church was destroyed, a result of the great damage from 1808 to 1814 by the French. Later walking by the river we ran into a familiar sight for folks from Arizona, Mormon Missionaries, one from Curitiba in Brazil and the other from the U.S. The Brazilian said "I couldn't understand a thing when I arrived" ["Não percebi nada quando vim"] so I did not feel so bad about the times I had trouble with the language in Portugal.

COIMBRA

The "Expresso" to Coimbra. The next day from Leiria we had tickets on an "express" bus which got on a "superhighway" to Coimbra, so we made good time. There was heavy pine forest much of the way and nice, occasional brick and tile country homes with pretty flower gardens in front as well as many vegetable gardens.

Coimbra served as the capital of Portugal in the Middle Age, but is best known for the university, the oldest in the Portuguese speaking world. The small city (third largest in population in Portugal but important beyond its size) has all the pre-requisites: Roman, Visigothic, Arab and finally Christian eras. It was conquered by Ferdinando de León to cement the beginning of the Christian era. Recall Portugal as a country only came into being in the 12th century and was previously a "Condado" or County of León in Old Castile. King Afonso Henriques is indeed buried in one of the old monasteries in the city. I was never quite sure where he ended up but was constantly reminded wherver we seemed to go that he got there first and captured whatever town or area from the Moslems!

Coimbra from the Mondego River

So Coimbra is an ancient town on the Mondego River and it looks the part. The convent and churches are on one skyline, the university on the other. The river is wide with the Santa Clara Bridge across it; the "centro" appears old and worn. It should. It took a while to warm to it after being in the several small towns the past few days. We had a fine lunch at the elegant "Dom Pedro" restaurant with a "maître" and several waiters ("senhores empregados"). Tour crowds were in.

"Portugal dos Pequenos" 1

"Portugal dos Pequenos" 2

Before walking the historic center of old Coimbra and up to the university, we did a curious outing across the river to "Portugal dos Pequenos"—"Portugal for the Children." In effect it was a tiny village with miniature castles of all the architectural types of Portugal, a bit of a playground for the tots, but also a history lesson for the adults. It was built during Salazar's "Estado Novo" and finished in 1950. We found it fun and mainly clever!

The University of Coimbra

Statue of Dom João III, Founder of the University of Coimbra, Mark

Camões in his "Lusiads" describes its founding in the 15th century, but it was actually founded by King Dinis in Lisbon in 1290, transferred to Coimbra in 1308, back to Lisbon a bit later and made permanent in 1537 in Coimbra when King João III initiated his own palace in the university. It attracted scholars and teachers from Oxford, Paris, Salamanca and Italy and was known as a Humanist University in its earliest days.

Originally known for the various religious faculties in the late Renaissance it became a center of science and scientific research due to the stimulous of the Marques de Pombal in the mid 18th century.

There are currently 7,500 students; they no longer wear the long black robes associated with past times but do attach colored ribbons designating their faculties to their briefcases. They are known, among other things, for playing guitar and singing "fados." They live communally in "repúblicas" of 12-13 students and hire a servant to cook for them. I recalled the same term and custom from days in Recife, Brazil, in the 1960s. The academic year ends in May with the "queima das fitas" or "the burning of the ribbons" of the graduates.

One enters the University by walking through the old city with the arches in its twelfth century walls and then climbing a very steep cobblestoned street. As mentioned, it was founded in the 12th century but basic work not done on it in until the 1500s by King João III (Avis) in 1537. Luís de Camões is an alumnus as well at St. Anthony of Pádua.

The "Biblioteca Geral"

Outside View of the Library of the University of Coimbra

The library constructed from 1717 to 1723 possesses the most elaborate interior architecture in all Portugal, all in the Baroque style.

Inside View of the Library of the University of Coimbra

It was a sight to see with the gilded baroque interior by King João V; it boasts one million tomes, jade and marble floors, gilded-lacquered walls and shelves, and painted scenes on the ceiling. It is a real art gallery in itself with gorgeous rosewood and ebony tables. It seems like it would be difficult to contentrate on work in the beginning with all this surrounding the reading table, but I would love to give it a try. The "Real Gabinete de Leitura" in Salvador and another in Rio de Janeiro are tropical efforts to match its grandeur, but they are of another age and although beautiful, not quite so glamorous.

The "Faculdade de Letras"

I had wanted to see the corresponding unit of the university to our "Department of Languages and Literatures" at Arizona State University; well, maybe not exactly since the entire system is different, following the European patterns. I had an encounter with Professor João Oliveira de Lopes, Professor of Brazilian Literature and "Literatura Popular do Nordeste" a course just taught in 1986-87. He was called at home, rushed over and we had a pleasant talk. He told of researching in Recife, knew Ariano Suassuna, Mário Souto Maior and Neuma Borges (personages of my research days in Brazil) and said all spoke well of me. He knew relatively little of Brazil's folk-popular literature, the "literatura de cordel," but I was impressed to know it was being taught at no less than Coimbra! He had used my 1973 book "A Literatura de Cordel" in the northeastern literature course.

Cultural note: a few years later at a conference in Recife, Brazil, one of the professors of the University of Lisbon spoke totally disparagingly of the "Universidade de Coimbra" as a Portuguese relic, totally out of step with modern days. It would be interesting to see today's dynamics between the Universities of Lisbon, Coimbra and O Porto. All I know is that the Universidade de Coimbra is the oldest in Portugal and dates from the times of the oldest in Europe including Paris, Salamanca, Alcalá de Henares and perhaps Bologna. It has earned its stripes!

"Igreja da Sé"—Coimbra

"Igreja da Sé" or Cathedral, Coimbra

On the "Via Latina" we saw the old "Igreja da Sé" or Cathedral of Coimbra. A curiosity was to see a man with one leg on crutches, carrying his wooden leg in a plastic sack. The old "Sé" was founded in 1170. It has a Romanesque portal and on the inside rounded arches and cupola; it was built like the fortress churches of the times all over Europe and was similar to the "Sé" in Lisbon but older. The "Sé" in Lisbon is Gothic; this is Romanesque.

The Altar of the "Igreja da Sé"

There was a gilded Flemish "retablo" above the main altar.

The Santa Cruz Church—Coimbra

We did not see this church but supposedly Afonso Henriques' sarcophagus is here, his feet resting on a lion. There is also reference to the scene of the climax of Pedro and Ines de Castro's story here.

Final Note on Tourism in Coimbra:

The Main Plaza of Coimbra

We walked through the downtown and to the railroad station and then across the river to the "Pinto D'Ouro" and our first disappointing supper from the Michelin Guide Book. The hotel was also really a sad story and put a bit of a damper on our stay due to icy cold water in the shower once again. But Coimbra grows on you and I think I could grow to like it with the river and its traditions. We saw only one person with the formerly required black academic gown at the university, no ribbons on it at all. All the students were in exam time; there were many hundreds of graduation pictures of them in the old robes on display throughout the campus.

Travel from Coimbra to the North of Portugal

    We were traveling on June 10th, Camões' Birthday, a National Holiday. After Coimbra I must say our trip to the North at this time began to take a downward spiral, but there were a few good moments and we did finally reach our goal—the cradle of Portuguese history in the small town of Guimarães in far northern Portugal. It all began when we did a five hour train ride to Viana do Castelo on the far northwestern shore of Portugal. We were up early in Coimbra and no cafés were open but we managed to get pastries for the trip. A very kind nun helped out with directions. The "comboio" or "elétrico" was a grubby electric line and was the milk run to O Porto. It was really quite inferior to the buses for you see so much less and the seats were straight back and stiff. We sat in first class by mistake. I could see no difference but the conductor moved us to second class. The train was filthy, uncomfortable and slow. A beggar lady with two small children with what we surmised were lice sat in front of Katie.

O PORTO

View of O Porto and the Douro River

Such was the scene from the train or highway overlooking the river. O Porto is on the right bank of the Douro; on the left is Vila Nova de Gaia with its famous wine houses and old ships with barrels on deck to transport the famous local wine, Port of course.

During the time of the Romans the two sites of the current cities were called "Portus" and "Cale," thus "Portucale," later to become "Portugal." In the eighth century the Moors invaded but never established themselves permanently. The region was a dowry of Princess Teresa, daughter of the King of Spanish León, to her husband Henri of Bergundy in 1095. The "Reconquista" of Portugal started from here and gave the name to the entire country.

VIANA DO CASTELO

The scenery in the North did not seem to be that much different; there were more small mountains, continuous vineyards; the latter are up in the air in arbor fashion with many crops planted below them. Many farmers, men and women, were hoeing weeds and working the fields. We saw few tractors. There were wheat, grapes, oats, fruit orchards and truck farms. The plots seemed small but the soil seemed rich and every inch was planted. In some ways it reminded me of Guatemala. The Portuguese peasants still surprised me; they had ruddy, Celtic looks while living and working like the Indians or Blacks I had seen in America.

View of Viana do Castelo and the Atlantic

The town dates from the 16th century when fishermen set out from here for the cod fishing off Newfoundland; the town still today thrives on deep sea fishing. It is in the province of Minho and is known for the folkloric dances in the month of August (we missed them). The funicular leads to the top of Santa Luzia Hill and church; from there the view of Viana do Castelo and the Lima Estuary is impressive. Of note are the 16th century central plaza and fountain. We arrived at the hotel, the most expensive thus far on our trip; it caters to tours from England. We ended having meals at "A Laranjeira" a great Portuguese Restaurant which reminded me of the old "A Portuguesa" in Salvador. We had two great meals there today: "empanadas, azeitonas, pão e manteiga, arroz à Valenciana, e omelete" first, and then "bife acebolado, batata frita, salada de legumes, vinho Rosé e verde." The cost for the first meal was about $5 each, $3.50 the second meal.

I liked "old" Viana with its 16th century plaza, fountains etc. The streets were narrow and cobblestoned with many shops. The town is on the Lima River and is perhaps three hundred yards from open sea. A sea wall breaks the waves. We took the funicular to the top of a local hill to Santa Luzia Church, a Renaissance beauty with a view of the area. Then it was back down the hill for ice cream, to the hotel and its "big screen, green tinted TV" where Katie saw a lot of junk and back to "A Laranjeira' for a good meal. We were ready for showers and bed and once again there was no hot water, keeping in mind the $50 per night tariff. It must have been the stress of many days on the road: I lost my temper and told the manager "Either hot water or a discount, and your hotel "é uma merda." They said they would resolve the issue the following a.m. It turned out to be no hot water and a $15 discount. Another disappointment was that we did not see any of the promised folklore (there were supposed to be folk costumes and dances of northern Portugal) but we did see the countryside from O Porto to the north and Viana is nice enough. On to Guimarães tomorrow.

June 11th

Viana do Castelo to Braga to Guimarães—Last Days of the Northern Tour

We took the local milk route bus to Braga through many small towns, school kids on and off, country women in black cape, blouse, etc. The road was windy throughout and it took one and one-half hours.

Braga is the capital of Minho. It was originally an old Roman town, then occupied by the Suevi in the 5th century, then the Visigoths, then the Moors, and finally the Portuguese during the Reconquest. The Roman Catholic Church was always important here, and Braga was once the seat of the Primate of All Spain! The holy days here are still important and pilgrims come from afar.

Bragança

Nearby on a high "serra" is the medieval city with ramparts. It was a Duchy in 1442. Here of course is the birthplace of the royal House of Bragança which renounced any claim to the Portuguese throne during the Spanish occupation of 1580-1640, but then reigned until 1910 and the popular revolution, the last royal house in Portugal. Note that the Braganças also ruled in Brazil from 1822 to 1889. The title of "Duke of Bragança" always meant the heir to the throne. The castle dates from 1187 and freedom from the Moors.

GUIMARAES

Guimarães is an historic city that had an important role in the formation of Portugal and was settled in the 9th century. The administrative seat of the "Condado de Portugal" or County of Portugal was established here by Henry of Bergundy. He was a knight who had gone in search of adventure in Hispania. He fought the Moors along with Alfonso VI of León. In honor of his contribution in the wars in Hispania, the King of León gave him the county of Portugal. He became Count of Portugal and his wife was Theresa, one of Alfonso VI's of León's daughters. In 1095 the County of Portugal was a dependency of the Kingdom of León. In 1097 after much fighting and history, Afonso Henriques, their son, would declare himself Prince and would rule the new country of Portugal.

Statue of Afonso Henriques, Founder of Portugal, Guimarães

Guimarães was the birthplace of Afonso I of Portugal, the first Portuguese King. And it was important because of the Battle of São Mamede in 1128. Forces led by Afonso Henriques defeated forces led by his mother Teresa of Portugal and her lover Fernão Peres de Trava. After winning, Afonso styled himself "Prince of Portugal." The capital would be moved to Coimbra in 1129. He would be called King of Portugal in 1139 and would be recognized as such by other countries in 1143.

Katie and Mark, Breakfast in the Hotel at Guimarães

There was some shock upon entering Guimarães because of a rattletrap city bus up to the hotel, our most expensive to this point in Portugal for $61 per night. But all in the room works well, and there is decent TV for the first time and with much programming in English (we saw "Alfred Hitchcock Presents" and "All in the Family"—how's that for the times?) And a bullfight from Spain!

We checked the train schedule and—uh oh!—there will be a train strike tomorrow. As George Clooney says in my favorite movie, "Oh Brother Where Art Thou?" we found ourselves "in a tight spot." We would be lucky to get an "expresso" bus at 10:20 the next day and be into Lisbon at 5 p.m. All this unfolded when I had left Keah and Katie at the Nicolino Restaurant, had walked to the train station of the "Rodoviaria Nacional," and found it to be closed due to the strike, and then lucked out to get the bus tickets. That morning also included a horrendous wait to change $100 at a bank; the bureaucracy never ceases here. Starved, we had a good lunch at the Nicolino— "Omelete, pão, etc."

The Castle of Guimarães

There was time for just a bit of tourism. We walked to the palace and castle of Guimarães. The former was founded in the 10th century and was finished by Afonso I the Duke of Bragança much later in 1401.

Stained Glass Windows, the Castle of Guimarães

It was a massive medieval type affair, beautifully restored with chapel, windows and thirty-nine chimneys!

Monastery from the Hill in Guimarães

Nearby was the "Igreja São Miguel do Castelo," 12th Century Romanesque. Afonso Henriques was "possibly" baptized there. Note that Afonso Henriques was contemporary to El Cid in Spain, just a bit younger.

Keah, Katie, Patio of the Monastery, Guimaráess

LISBON ANEW

June 12th

After the all important tourism of Guimarães, the "Cradle of Portugal" and birthplace of Afonso Henriques, then there was the bus past O Porto, Coimbra and into Lisbon and its traffic jams. The last night would bring dinner once again at the "Bom Jardim."

June 13th.

Last trip in Portugal—the Bus from Lisbon to the Border of Spain

This was our last day in Portugal. We had a nice tour bus for the trip heading south and east beginning with a view of the "Rio Tejo" from the bridge, the huge statue of the "Cristo Redentor" and a freeway to Setubal. Then we entered the countryside where we saw olive and cork trees, rolling hills and wheat fields, sheep, and occasional vineyards, but the latter were not like those in abundance on the high roads in the North. When the wheat is cut they make bales of straw. The olive orchards were everywhere with castles on the hills in the distance. This was quintessential rural Portugal! For that matter we would see the same in western and southern Spain on the way to Málaga.

We passed through Évora, 47 kilometers south on our highway, past the Castle of Estremoz and its fame of King Dom Dinis of the 1400s and his wife Isabella who became a saint. There was a legend of her giving gold to the poor; he discovered it and the gold turned to roses. She was from Aragón. They used to say, "Poor Diniz."

All this was in great contrast to Lisbon, its coast and the north. The landscape was now colored gold and brown, there was little traffic and the roads were good. At one point in Elvas we saw a great aqueduct three stories high, first evidence of the Roman occupation of what would become Portugal thus the Roman term "Lusitânia."

From Lisbon to the Spanish border it is 226 kilometers via Setubal, Évora and Elvas. From the border it is 425 kilometers to Madrid. At the border the bus agent collected passports and we sat and waited. There was time to nap.

FINAL THOUGHTS ON PORTUGAL

So like the classes at the university, as we end this "class," perhaps a review of the Royal Dynasties of Portugal is a good thing:

Afonso Henriques is a son of Henry of Bergundy and Teresa of Castile-León (1130-1158). The Bergundians would rule until the Avis Dynasty.

The Avis' dynasty (1385-1580) had come in after defeating Spain in 1385 at Aljubarrota after Spain had claimed the Portuguese crown when there was no Portuguese successor. João I (Avis) takes over and the Avis dynasty will continue until 1580. That is when King Sebastião goes to Morocco and has the ill-fated battle and meets his demise.

With no successor Spain claims the throne again and will rule for 60 years until 1640. The restoration on that date is of course marked by the "Monumento dos Restauradores" in Lisbon. The Braganças come in the 1640s after the Restoration and would rule until 1910 with the assassination in 1908 and exile in 1910.

More Final Thoughts on Portugal

So keeping in mind all this history, I mentally reviewed why we started this trip to the Iberian Peninsula in Portugal. I had wanted to see the main sights, but always with an eye to Portugal's seafarers and discoverers, its history and its major writers. We succeeded in that although only these notes and the slides recall it to mind. I never taught "Portuguese" Portuguese, only studied a survey of its literature and really only read seriously Camões and a novel or two of Eça de Queróz of the 19th century. This short time did fill in many gaps. But back home at Arizona State University it was all an emphasis on Brazil. The travel, the tourist sites, the food and wine, and hearing that continental Portuguese were other highlights of the trip. The accommodations and that icy water in the showers put a bit of a damper on travel. In retrospect it was worth it all; Mark, Keah and Katie built a lot of character and as I said, "a little suffering is good." There was far more pleasure in seeing those wonderful sights and thinking of the great sea farers and poets!

PART II

TRAVEL AND TEACHING IN SPAIN

This narrative will combine notes from the days of teaching in the summer school in Spain (very few notes, as mentioned, it was what happened outside the classroom or tutorial that was important) and general tourism. I have taken care to add notes on the history of each place and the literary figures associated with them, the latter memorable from the courses taken at Saint Louis University and later taught at ASU. There will be many pictures of the social gatherings and parties as we did indeed socialize in Spain! The evenings with the Flys and friends and students really counter balanced all that history and tourism and certainly provided the lighter moments.

June 13th

TRAVEL FROM PORTUGAL TO MÁLAGA AND LIFE IN MÁLAGA

There were wheat fields, olive orchards, cattle and emptiness through much of Badajoz. We passed through the Sierra Morena of "Don Quixote" fame with winding roads and more olive groves, down through the Guadalquivir Valley and past Sevilla where we saw La Giralda from the highway.

Then there was a long, long stretch of wheat, olive groves, vineyards and "gira-soles" or huge sunflowers in the flat and low rolling hills, and finally barren mountains before the descent into Málaga and a view of the Mediterranean Ocean.

We took a taxi to the hostel and were reunited with Miguel, Felisa and Tamara Flys and enjoyed dinner with them.

Málaga Harbor and "Plaza de Toros"

Málaga is a city and a municipality, capital of the Province of Málaga in the modern parlance "Autonomous Community of Andalusia." One of the oldest cities in the western world, it was founded by the Phoenicians and was under the power of ancient Carthage! It then came under Roman rule and after them Islamic domination for eight hundred years. In 1487 it came under Christian rule again. It is perhaps best known in modern times as the birthplace of Pablo Picasso. Yours truly can attest to its amazing Spanish Classic Guitar heritage with the entire Romero family which was forced to migrate from Málaga during Franco days to the United States. We have the Generalísimo to thank for this!

June 14th

    The next morning there was breakfast of "pan de molde" and "café con leche" then mass at the Cathedral of Málaga. The cathedral was huge, a combination of Romanesque, Gothic and Baroque. Then there was a big lunch of "menu del día" and a siesta. We took a taxi to the sea shore of Málaga to the Parador Gibralfaro and its Alcazaba with a nice view of the port, then to bed around one a.m. Dinner that night was with the students at the Pizza Capri.

June 15th

    We took a bus to school, had the first class and I gave my introduction to "Don Quixote." I was excited about this. There was a snack with John Griggs, Joseph, Sharon and Mike, then the bus home. Lunch was at the "Restaurante Gallego:" "caldo gallego y rosbif."

Tamara and Katie on the "Burrico" in the Park

We took Katie and Tamara to the "Paseo Público" park in Málaga for play. The donkey is made of metal and its ears are shiny from all that rub the brass for good luck. Keah and I had a nice walk along the quay to the Parola and Malagueta area of beach and the ocean. We noted the big billboards with advertisements for the upcoming "Feria" or Festival. Then it was time to returne "home" for a snack and impromptu party in Flys' room.

June 16th

The next morning brought serious study and preparation for the Quixote class in the morning.

Beach Scene at Torremolinos, Miguel, Felisa, Katie and Keah

That noon we hopped a bus with the Flys and Hills to Torremolinos—the town and the beach. The bus ride was totally unimpressive; the countryside was dry, brown, bleak and with lots of trash along the highway until we entered the town. Once we arrived at the ocean then there was a resort atmosphere all the way. I cannot compare the scene and experience to the French or Italian Riviera but suspect they are quite similar. The atmosphere exudes sun, sex and pleasure! What else? The beach was brown sand and with rock pebbles, not quite what I was used to in Acapulco or the shores of Brazil, but the water was a beautiful turquoise, calm with nary a wave, incredibly so for a "sea."

Currans on the Paddleboat, Torremolinos

There were paddle boats like on the Russian Postcards of the Black Sea Resorts. The water was icy cold! I did get in all the way but could not bear it for long, so it was no fun to swim. The big story for us was that the beach was topless! Indeed we saw some nice boobs, mainly English and Scandinavian I think, judging from the top of the head down! Our female students were a bit reluctant to join in!

My stomach was upset so at lunch I had Spanish "tortilla" or potato, good for the stomach they say. Later we all had huge "sangria" drinks and watched an entire bullfight on television. It was a good TV introduction to Spain! We returned home to the hostel and had "tapas" and wine in Professor Flys' room. Katie loved the beach!

June 17th. Wed.

I felt a bit rocky in the a.m., read for school and "Don Quixote" day two. We were home at noon and a nap; then I waited for one of the young coed students whom I would tutor on Spanish grammar. There was a late lunch at the local Pizza Capri, good pizza.

The "Sevillanas" Show at the "Malagueta" Festival

That p.m. we all went to the "Malagueta" festival with the ladies in flamenco-style dresses, a street dance atmosphere, but now with the true "ambiente" of Spain! This now seemed to be what we expected to see - the "real" Spain! It was impressive! Part of the "feria" or "fiesta" would be the series of major bullfights held in Spain at the Malagueta arena.

Statues of Jesus and Mary at Málaga Cathedral

June 18th

Keah, Katie and I attended mass at the Cathedral with its statues of the Black Christ and the elegant Virgin Mary, organ music, singing and afterwards the huge Corpus Christi procession. The Cathedral dates from the 16th century and the choir and choir stalls in beautifully carved wood come from the 17th. That morning for the mass the Cathedral was jammed, the only time we have seen that thus far on the trip. The priest droned on for about fifty minutes about Corpus Christi and Caritas! The P.A. system was good, and his Spanish was slow and beautiful, the clearest I have heard here—that of an "Obispo." The organ in the Málaga Cathedral was nice and there was some singing as well.

The Monstrance for the Corpus Christi Procession

We left mass early not because of the clarity of the priest's diction but due to the previously alluded to fifty minute sermon. Outside the church doors we were facing the Bishop's palace in front of the cathedral and saw the huge silver and gold monstrance carried in the Corpus Christi procession. Thousands of people were milling about, winding through the downtown area in the procession. There was a military band, banners, priests and mainly the monstrance. I surmise this is a bit like Holy Week or "Semana Santa."

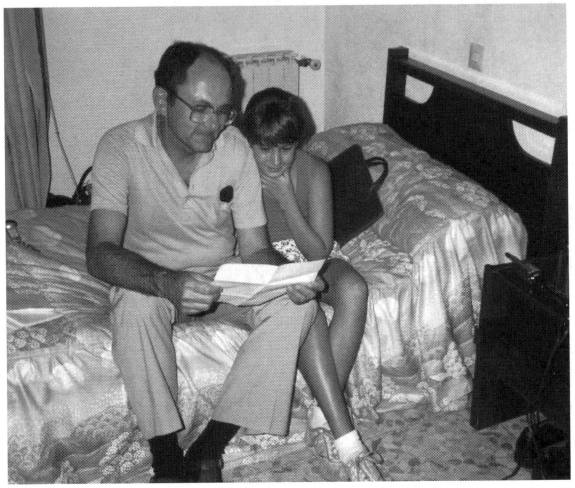

Father's Day in Málaga

A bit of personal life perhaps may be permitted; even in far off Spain the Currans and Katie continued a family tradition—the Father's Day card and celebration.

"Malagueta" Festival: Horsemen and Their Ladies

Another aspect of the "Malagueta" Festival which we were indeed fortunate to see was in the streets where there were beautiful Andalusian horses with the "caballeros" in their flat brimmed hats and the ladies riding side saddle in their flamenco dresses.

Two Arabians and "Caballeros"

This of course is the area of Spain famous for blue blooded horses and people who know how to train and ride them. The famous Arabians!

The "Corrida de Toros" in Málaga

"Toreros" Arrive in Style to the Arena

We saw the "toreros" for the bull fight in their "traje de luces" arriving in carriages on the way to the Plaza. This was a major event, but at some point of time in Málaga we went to a small-time amateur bullfight featuring the "escuela taurina" or bullfighting academy. It was a school for both the students and very young bulls—these were the real stock but were not full grown and heavy and their horns were filed down. The music was the accustomed of the bull fight and was moving in that sense.

The "Malagueta" arena is "classic" in shape with "small" boxes on the upper decks and the "sol y sombra" section on concrete steps below. The crowd was tiny, the "picador" was used only slightly; no one could get the "banderillas" placed. A young girl or "toreadora" came in and was tossed by the bull on the first "paso." This amateur experience perhaps gives perspective to one of the serious ones I had the good fortune to see in of all places along the Mexico-U.S. border in Arizona, i.e. el Cordobés en Nogales, México.

An aside is permitted on bull fighting with the premise that this author is by no means an expert, but I am a fan. I've seen the old classic black and white film on "El Gran Manolete" and others, but for my generation the most famous "torero" in all Spain was "El Cordobés." One of the best books I have seen on the art of bull fighting is "Or I'll Dress You in Mourning" and is the biography of El Cordobés. Notwithstanding accounts by Ernest Hemingway, Gerald Brenan or Michener, it is like nothing else I have ever read and I recommended it in every Spanish culture class I taught at the university. To make a long story short, at the height of his success El Cordobés was enticed by some wealthy entrepreneurs to bring his talents to Mexico, but to an unusual venue—he was hired to do a series of bullfights in various border town arenas in the late 1960s - Ciudad Juárez, Nogales, Arizona, and Tijuana in California among them. It was in Nogales just a three hour drive from Tempe and the University that I and friends witnessed a true spectacle. Not only did he shine that afternoon, receiving six ears if I am not mistaken, but did something that forever is in my mind: he did a series, many "pasos" or passes on his knees with his back to the bull, an unimaginably daring feat.

That night in Málaga we were exhausted, but showered and dressed and went down to the "Malagueta" Festival again. This time there was blaring, unbearable disco music on the main street and blaring "sevillana" and "flamenco" music elsewhere—it was a true street dance in southern Spain. There were dozens of girls in flamenco dresses dancing with the men, all doing graceful "sevillanas," a dance it was a real pleasure to watch. Katie loved it all and is a joy, but just exhausts herself. She loves Málaga, the beach, Tamara and the students (the young college age coeds spoil her and Tamara a bit).

GRANADA

Travel to Granada and the Alhambra cannot be separated from the literature associated with the area. Throughout this text I shall mention, at least briefly, the famous names of Spanish Literature linked to the places we will see. The text is meant to be just a "vignette" of each; after all, we are not in Curran's Spanish Literature class! But some of the greats of Andalucía were as follows:

Luis de Góngora, 1561-1622, was born in Córdoba with later studies at the renowned University of Salamanca and then life in the court in Madrid. He became Spain's most famous poet of the Baroque Age, part of Spain's "Siglo de Oro." His most famous book of poetry is "Las Soledades." He was considered "the prince of darkness" or "el príncipe de las tinieblas" for the obscurity of his difficult verse, but I was "versed" in Góngora by Dr. Edward Sarmiento from Saint Louis University days with many long hours of study in the library. Í took great pride in understanding much of his verse.

El Duque de Rivas, 1791-1865, was one of the most famous of the Spanish Romanticists. His play "Don Álvaro o la fuerza del sino" ["Don Álvaro or the Force of Destiny"] is one of the masterpieces of the Romantic period and was of course later adapted by the Italians to a famous opera "La Forza del Destino." He was born in Córdoba, studied at Cádiz and later played a major role in the Liberal Cortes of 1814. Then along with other liberals he was exiled in France and returned to Madrid in later years.

Federico García Lorca was born in Fuentevaqueros a small town outside of Granada. He was a student and poet at the famous "Residencia de Estudiantes" in Madrid, later traveled performing folk drama through Spain (there is a real parallel in Brazil with Ariano Suassuna and colleagues' "Teatro do Estudante de Pernambuco" when they set as a goal the performance of theater for the masses in the tiny plazas of northeastern Brazil in the 1950s), ventured to New York City to write some wild verse, and then returned to Spain only to face death in 1936. Legend has it, but contested, his death was attributed directly to the Falange of Francisco Franco. But his gypsy, flamenco flavored poetry has no equal in Spain. I taught and re-taught "Romance Sonámbulo" in the survey courses for many years.

Tourism

We traveled by bus through rolling hills and low mountains with cork and olive trees and lots of wheat into Granada. It was a very impressive and large bustling city. There are two rivers in the valley, so farming and orchards are healthy, including many orange groves.

The Three Hills of Granada

The city is built on a "vega" or plain with three hills surrounding it with the Sierra Nevada to the southeast with one peak above 11,000 feet which the tourist brochures say has snow year around. The three hills surrounding the city of Granada are the Albaicín, Sacramonte with the gypsy caves and la Alhambra itself. Granada was a provincial capital when Córdoba was the seat of the Moorish Caliphate and was the capital of the "Almorávides" kingdom which overran the city of Granada in the 11th century. Granada, in turn, reached its full glory with the "Nasrides" kingdom from the 13th to the 15th centuries. In the latter times the Moorish rulers paid tribute to the Spanish kings of Navarra, León and Castile to leave them alone. Córdoba's nobility had fled and migrated to Granada when Catholic Spain took Córdoba in the 13th century.

The Nasrides ruled in the 13th, 14th and 15th centuries, but quarreled in the 15th under the Spanish threat. The Alhambra itself was built in the 14th century.

Legend or fact this is the tale they tell: the Caliph of Granada was in love with a Christian girl, this in the 15th century. His mother the queen fled with him from Granada; they later returned and deposed the king his father and thus put the son on the throne. There were quarrels amongst the Nasrides and a massacre at Abencerrajes by the Moorish rivals during this period. Then the Spanish King Fernando de Aragón seized the boy king. The Catholic Kings arrived in 1492, and the boy king Boabdil and the mother queen handed over the city and went into exile. Thus the saying arose, "Weep like a woman over what you could not defend as a man."

THE ALHAMBRA

One Moorish king destroyed the palace of his predecessors and then built his own palace upon the ruins, using the rubble and rocks for the new walls. Interior decoration was most important with all the rooms facing interior patios. The exterior walls were excessively plain. The interior décor is in fact stuccowork—finely modeled plaster in intricate patterns with low relief to catch the light and with built up layers akin to stalactites. The effect is called the "mocárabes." There are ceramic tiles on most interior walls, the "azulejos."

One enters through the Pomegranate Gate built by Carlos V, Hapsburg King of Spain, after the fall of Granada. To one side is the "Alcazaba" the military part.

To the other side is the "Alcázar" or palace from the 14th century; this was in effect the "Casa Real" of the Nasrides.

One enters the palace through the "Mexuar," the former council chamber transformed into a chapel by the Spaniards after 1492. From there one has a wonderful view of the Albaicín quarter. One then can see the Mexuar Court with the pool.

"La Corte de los Arrayanes—La Alhambra"

Then one sees the "Corte de los Arrayanes" (Mrytles) colonnaded at each end with the pool in the center.

Arches in the "Barca" Gallery

Other features are the Comares Towers and the Barca Gallery.

Another famous room is the Hall of the Ambassadors. This was the audience chamber of the Moorish Kings. It faced the throne. It was domed with cedar wood in a "Mudéjar" ceiling with paneled horseshoe arches and windows on three sides. Ceilings were decorated in stucco and walls with azulejos with more than 150 patterns in this room alone.

"El Patio de los Leones"

The "Patio de los Leones" was done in the 14th century by Mohammed V and is the heart of the palace. There are delicate, colonnaded arcades surrounded by the fountain and the pool.

"El Salón de las Dos Hermanas"

In the "Salón de las Dos Hermanas" there is a honeycombed, stucco ceiling which is difficult to capture, even on film. This was perhaps my favorite, and that is difficult to say, of all the rooms in the Alhambra.

The "Generalife"

"El Patio del Generalife"

This complex is connected to the Alhambra palace by a serious of patios and corridors. In the exterior of the Alhambra there are gardens leading to baths—the gardens are stepped and were used as though a gemstone, all with gravity flow.

This was the summer palace of the kings with its incredible terraced gardens, cypress, irrigation, pools, fountains and a view back to the Alcázar. "Los cipreses" [cypress] and "las adelfas" [flowering oleander!] were impressive. My colleague in Spanish at ASU, John Knowlton, a poet and student of great poets, told of relaxing in the gardens and perhaps even writing a poem or two! He was forever inspired by the verse of García Lorca and I can just image him sitting quietly by the fountain and reciting "Romance Sonámbulo" in a dramatic voice. He was certainly the most poetically inspired of all our professors at A.S.U. We spent many an hour at A.S.U. baseball games in the springtime in Tempe but talked mostly of Spanish Literature and our times in Spain.

Flowers and Fountains of "El Generalife"

The palace is surrounded by the elongated court. There is the "Patio de la Acequía" or "Canal Court"—beautiful! And there is a "Mirador" which overlooks the city of Granada and the Darío Valley.

The Palace of Carlos V in Granada

It was started in 1526 and was to be financed by a tax on the Moors. There was an uprising in 1568 which stopped construction. It is purely Classical in architecture, a good example of Renaissance art and architecture in Spain. It was done by Pedro Machuca who studied under Miguel Ángelo. One of its traits is huge, circular patio within the square building.

The Royal Chapel ["La Capilla Real"]

It was begun by the architect Egas in 1506 and was completed by Carlos V in 1526 in part based on the decision of the Catholic Kings ["Los Reyes Católicos"] to be buried at the site of the final "Reconquista" and not at Toledo which was their main residence at the time. It is in Isabelline style with ribbed vaulting and coats of arms of the monarchs of the Trastamara linage: a single Águila (not the double eagle of the Hapsburgs).

A screen is placed in front of the chapel thus providing "rejas;" inside is the mausoleum of the Catholic Kings, the first design from 1517 in Genoa, the second in 1519-20 by a Spaniard. The sarcophagi are all below in the crypt. Isabella la Católica's personal art collection and her crown as well and Fernando's sword are in an adjoining room

The Cathedral of Granada

"Santiago Matamoros," Royal Chapel, Granada

It was constructed in the 16th and 17th centuries. The rotunda is surrounded by the ambulatory and both are linked to the Nave and four aisles of the Basilica. It is massive with 16th century stained glass. It seemed huge and "colder" than the cathedral of Málaga. This is but one of its gilded altars. One can only assume it depicts Spain's patron saint, "Santiago Mata Moros!"

The Modern City of Granada

It seemed much more of a true metropolis than Málaga. I wrote, "This place has a lot to offer." In spite of not being on the sea, it is much more interesting for its history and art and seemed more attuned to Spain rather than to tourists.

We returned "home" to Málaga via the bus, enjoyed "tapas" in the room and dinner with Joe, Mike, Sharon, John Griggs, Miguel, Felisa, Tamara and us.

"La Bodega" and "Jamón Serrano," Málaga

After our return to Málaga, we went to the "Ultramarino" market in the a.m. I managed to fit in the Granada notes and Quixote study. Later we went to the fruit market—you don't touch or pick over the fruit here! Meat is sold by ¼ kilo or 150 grams or ½ kilo, etc. We bought fruit, meats, wine and bread for the coming picnic. With the things from the market there was a nice picnic lunch, a local custom, with the usual crowd at the Hostel. There was one problem—one student got lost in Granada, is on the phone and Michael Flys was up to 4 a.m. with him.

There was some tension about all of us going to the "Aqua Park," etc. Thinking this is a "Spanish water park and slide," Keah and I opted to go to the old plaza of Málaga for the "contest of horses and carriages" ["concurso de caballos y enganche"] with Andalusian Thoroughbreds, all Arabic horses and high steppers. The costumes were great, including those of the drivers, coachmen, "caballeros" on horses with flat Andalusian hats and ladies in flamenco-style dresses riding side saddle. Sorry. It beat the water park.

In those days and nights in Málaga there was always great music and regional dances for hours in the "Paseo Público" with dance troupes doing "sevillanas, rondas, y granadinas" which are dances and dance steps from all of Andalusia. It was a real treat and was very enjoyable: the femininity of the girls, their carriage and their beautiful dresses. It was this fiesta which has highlighted our days in Málaga.

June 21st, Sunday

Keah, Katie and I went once again to the Cathedral with a mass in clear Spanish, and we sat in the "coro" or choir carved in gorgeous wood from the 17th century and heard the thundering classical organ music during the mass. It was a very nice experience in the old church with us sitting in the same seats as the monks of the old days. There was a huge carved 17th century music stand for the Gregorian antiphonaries. Clouds of incense filled the air. It was a good experience.

This was followed by another outing to Torremolinos and the beach this p.m. This time we took the RENFE or electric commuters' train; it was dirty, slow and crowded. Highlights were lunch and drinks followed by one of the students losing her purse to a pickpocket, a tourist curse I shall write more about later. But there remained the beach and topless attractions and icy water.

June 22nd

There was study and a good Quixote class in the a.m., a lunch of "paella" across the street, rest and reading in the p.m. and a "paseo" to . . .

THE ALCAZABA OR MOORISH PALACE OF MÁLAGA

The Moorish "Alcazaba," Katie, Málaga

It is built upon Phoenician and Roman ruins. There is a museum of Moorish art; the place is a bit in time before Granada. There was a nice view from the parapet looking at the Port of Málaga. We then went to the "Paseo Público" in the shopping area; a flamenco dress costs $200 U.S. with none of the accoutrements; we opted out perhaps to Katie's dismay but evened things up with a beautiful Lladró image of a young Flamenco dancer purchased later in Madrid. That evening there was talk and dinner of "sopa de gallina" at the Capri. Between the loss of some students' documents and the unbalanced student stranded in Granada, it was a busy and hectic time. Teaching "Don Quitote" was a calming distraction for me and the tutorial with the student in the grammar class was fine for the moment.

That evening there was a nice outing to San Juan de Palo, a fishing village outside Málaga. It featured a big meal on the beach—we tried "chilos" or clams, shrimp, salad, and wine. It was nice on the beach as we watched the boats and the big "hogueras" or bonfires. Later there was a drink at the corner bar before going home; Mark had "coñac," the only time in Spain.

June 24th.

Katie was sick in the night with fever, chills, and diarrhea (there are two bugs going around—horrible throat with cold and stomach and fever). Keah and I are okay so far; we bought antibiotics today in case of emergency. June 25th. Keah is caring for Katie; Mark takes off alone for the bus trip to Mijas, Fuengirola and the view along the sea.

MIJAS

The Burros of Mijas

Streets, Houses and Flowers, Mijas

This is a tourist town set up by the tourist agencies to be a "pueblo típico de Andalucía." Set on the side of a small mountain, it presented a view toward Fuengirola overlooking the Mediterranean Coast. The streets of Mijas were narrow and steep with whitewashed houses, grill work on windows and flowers nearby. The ride home to Málaga was on the "milk run" with an old, rickety bus. I traveled with a tour group from Tampa, Florida, and some Cuban Americans. The winding road parallels the coast; we saw beautiful "villas" with swimming pools with views. We eventually ended in Torremolinos but coming in the back way past the ole' Aqua Park and Tivoli Park.

June 26th. DAY TRIP TO CÓRDOBA

The Roman Bridge at Córdoba

Córdoba rests on the west bank of the Guadalquivir River. Its history goes way back, all the way to Roman Baética in 152 B.C when it shortly thereafter became the Roman capital of Hispania; we noted the Roman Bridge over the river. All was compressed into a day trip, intensive but great! The town is inseparable from its literary figures: this was the birthplace of both Sénecas from the first century A.D.: Séneca the Rhetorician of 55 B.C. and his son Lucas Séneca the philosopher and Preceptor of Nero from 4 B.C. to 65 A.D. According to one source Nero named him a Consul and also commanded him to commit suicide! Lucanus of Córdoba was a companion to Nero. As mentioned earlier, centuries later in safer times, relatively speaking, the Spanish Baroque poet and "prince of darkness" Luis de Góngora was from here as well.

In 719 A.D. the Emirs from the Damascus Caliphate migrated here and set up a new caliphate. The Umayyad dynasty would rule for 300 years with great prosperity and high culture. In 929 A.D. the caliphate in Spain is declared independent from Damascus. In 1000 the caliphate crumbles into what became separate Moorish Kingdoms—the "Taifas." The area was called "Al Andalus." Córdoba then fell under the rule of Sevilla until the 12th century when the Christians conquered.

The Scholar Maimónides, Córdoba

In 1126 to 1198 it is the time of the Moorish scholar Averroes, famous for his learning and for the teachings and writings of Aristotle he brought to the West. Then it is the time of Maimónides 1135-1204: a Jewish scholar of medicine and philosophy. An aside: the guidebook said there are only 15,000 Jews in modern Spain.

Cristóbal Colón received permission here in Córdoba from the "Reyes Católicos" to do the voyage to the West. "El Gran Capitán," Gonzalo Fernández de Córdoba (1453-1515) was the general of the Catholic Kings who carried out the conquest of Córdoba and later captured Naples as well in 1504.

"La Mesquita de Córdoba"

It was the high point of Caliphate art begun in the middle of the 8th century, augmented by later kings and finished in the 10th century.

"La Puerta del Perdón," "La Mesquita," Córdoba

One enters through "La Puerta del Perdón" and enters the Court of the Orange Trees ["Naranjos"]. The outside of the mosque is plain with a brick wall. There were fountains and baths to wash in, thus purifying oneself before entering the temple—the best known called the Al Mansur Basin.

The mosque is overlooked by the Minaret; we climbed its stairway to see a great view of the river and the city from there. The Arabs bought the location, razed the old Visigothic Christian church and began building in many phases: 785, 848, 961 and 987.

They used the old marble columns from previous churches and raised in the Mesquita a massive number of columns. These are double arched (one arch on top of the other; the red and white color is from the stone alternated with red brick). The original aisles were open to the court. The Christians closed in the arches later.

Entrance to the "Mihrab" Córdoba

The Mihrab

This is the highly ornamented chapel of the Caliphs, similar in style to that seen in the Alhambra but done years earlier.

The Silver Hapsburg Double Eagle, the Catholic Cathedral in "La Mesquita"

In the 16th century during the reign of Carlos V in 1523 the Spaniards cut away the center of the Mosque to build the Cathedral vault and cupola. When Carlos V saw this in the 1520s he was shocked and dismayed and stopped further construction. It was completed later. The Church is Gothic (1520-1547), Renaissance (the 1560s) and Italian (1598).

The Alabaster Bull and Pulpit, The Catholic Cathedral in "La Mesquita de Córdoba"

The dome and the Baroque choirs with pulpits which date from 1760 are all done in dark mahogany. This was the same wood as used in the pulpit.

The great irony: the Christian practice during the "Reconquista" was to destroy all mosques and build Catholic cathedrals in their place. This great mosque was saved only because the Catholic Cathedral was built inside. History is a witness to its uniqueness: two faiths under one roof. It was impressive for its size, the beauty of Moslem design and also the combination of Christian designs in the cathedral. For me (after seeing the Alhambra) it was the contrast that made it most interesting.

The Jewish Quarter of Córdoba

The Jewish Quarter and Its Flowers, Katie, Córdoba

We enjoyed and admired it—the narrow streets, the whitewashed walls, the great interior patios with flowers. The Jews were thrown out of Spain in 1492.

We did not see the "Playa de Potro" and the inn described in "Don Quixote."

All in all Córdoba was impressive. We had a great lunch with the students—a "plato combinado" followed by a hot climb up to the Minaret with its views. We got a bit dizzy when the bell rang in our ears.

SEVILLA

June 27th "La Gira" Continues to Sevilla

At this point in the first phase of the summer school, classes and time around Málaga concluded and we began phase two, an incredible travel trip which would take us to northern and northwestern Spain and finally back down through "Castilla la Vieja" to Madrid. Our first outing was northwest to Sevilla. Our tourism in that compressed time included visits to the Cathedral, the Alcázar, la Giralda, the River Guadalquivir, and the Plaza de España. On a lesser cultural note there was lunch at the "Hamburger Alameda," a nap, a short jaunt back to the Cathedral for mass, and that night to the Patio Sevillana and a flamenco show.

History: Sevilla Capital of "Andalucía"

A cultural note before more serious matters: the great Romantic poet Gustavo Adolfo Bécquer was born here before aspiring to and and then livng life in Madrid. He was known for his book "Rimas" in the 19th century. The straight forward verse is among my favorites in Spanish poetry.

The "Torre de Oro" on the Guadalquivir was built in 1220 to guard the port; it had a chain hooked to the other side of the river to stop boats from passing upriver.

Sevilla was already converted to Christianity when the Alhambra was being built, but chose to maintain the "Mudéjar" style. It was originally an Iberian town, later a Roman capital until it was replaced by Toledo in 711 with the conquest by the Arabs. When Córdoba fell to the Almóhades, Sevilla was made a Moorish capital from 1184-1197. The Almóhades king defeated the Christians in 1195 and he built the Giralda; originally it was a minaret. In 1248 King Fernando III of Castile defeats the Moors.

In 1492 Cristóbal Colón sets out on the voyage to what would become "the New World" from Sevilla. Note that Américo Vespucci, 1451-1512, wanted to prove what Columbus had discovered was not the East Indies or its islands but a new continent. In 1500 the Portuguese adventurer Pedro Álvares Cabral, perhaps blown off course, would repeat Columbus's feat: stumbling into a land mass that would later become Brazil. Also a bit later came the Portuguese's Magalhães' voyage around the world in 1519.The sole survivor, one of his captains, was Juan Elcano who returned in 1521.

In 1503 Isabella la Católica had created the "Casa de Contratación" in Sevilla to maximize control of the Indies. The records from those times are in the "Archivo de Indias" in Sevilla. Sevilla remained the main port until 1717 when the river silted up and the monopoly passed to

Cádiz. A modern historic note: in 1936 the Falange and the "Nacionalistas" led by Francisco Franco started their revolt here in Sevilla.

The Monuments

"La Giralda (the Old Mosque) de Sevilla"

"La Giralda" was begun in the 12th century as a minaret for the Arabs. The top was only completed in the 16th century. It is 230 feet to the top; there are 35 levels of gradual incline. There is a legend that says that Isabella la Católica would ride her horse to the top for the view.

"La Catedral de Sevilla"

Huge Entry Door, the Cathedral of Sevilla

The edifice is massive, thus conjuring the old saying: "We will build a cathedral so immense they will call us madmen." It is third in size of all of Europe, after St. Paul's in London and St. Peter's in Rome. It is 184 feet high on the inside, has a Gothic and Renaissance exterior, with interior columns and vaulting.

The Tomb of Columbus Carried by the Four Kings of Spain

Whether Columbus is still there is quite another matter. Naples in Italy and Santo Domingo in the Dominican Republic as well as Sevilla claim him.

The Silver Monstrance, Cathedral of Sevilla

We have already seen the huge silver monstrance of the Cathedral of Málaga on the occasion of the Corpus Christi Procession. This one tops it in appearance if not value. And yet another, of some thirty-seven kilos of gold, is in the Cathedral of Sevilla (photos were prohibited, sorry). Should one of the curious readers of this book not be Catholic, a short non-academic explanation might be in order. In Roman Catholic liturgy, the exposition of the Blessed Sacrament, the Sacred Host which Catholics believe to be the very body of Jesus Christ, in an appropriate "home" or "housing" became essential during the Benediction Services, particularly during Lent. The "home" is known as a monstrance. If you follow the logic, Christ must be placed in the finest, the most elegant, the richest of "homes" (in effect the home away from home—the accepted resting place in the churches is called the Holy Tabernacle. Like the monstrance, it too might be encased in gold.) One can see that non-believers might consider all this as ostentatious particularly when one knew that the gold or silver was mined on the backs of Indian or Black Slaves in the New World. The Liberals of the 19th century finally caught up with all this in excoriating the church in Spain and Latin America and doing their best to separate it from its riches. President Benito Juárez in Mexico, a full blooded Zapotec Indian brought up and cared for when young by the Church is a good example. We have witnessed such finery in the country of Colombia, but locked in bank vaults save for the militaryily guarded Holy Week processions. One might add that a good deal of the gold from the mines of America was used by the Spanish Crown to pay its debts to bankers and rival nations of Europe.

But we do have personal photos of guilded altars and statues, among them . . .

Statue of the Virgin, Cathedral of Sevilla

The main altar or "Retablo Mayor" of Sevilla's Cathedral is Flemish from the late 1400s to early 1500s. It is massive in gold leaf and with painted scenes. It is the largest of its type in Spain and is impressive for the color and complexity. Only Toledo is its rival. Alas, again, we have no personal photos, only the commercial slides which cannot be reproduced here. But other lesser examples do appear later in the book. It is worth the time to "google" the matter to see the photos.

The Alcázar of Sevilla

Entrance to the "Alcázar," Sevilla

It is unique in that it was built by a Christian King, Pedro el Cruel, from 1350 to 1369, but all originally in "Mudéjar" style, copying the style of the Alhambra. The Catholic Kings later added on quarters for the personnel of the "Casa de Contratación" the primary bureaucratic entity governing commerce in the New World discovered by Christopher Columbus and conquered by Hernán Cortés, Hernando Pizarro and many others.

Inside the "Alcázar," Interior Ornamentation

Moorish Interior Décor, the "Alcázar"

Queen Isabella's quarters done in 1504 were modeled on the "Mexuar" of the Alhambra. The newest part is the court of Carlos V, Renaissance style. As in Córdoba, nearby is the "Barrio Judío" with narrow streets and patios. It is called the "Barrio de Santa Cruz."

Entrance to King Carlos V's Palace, Sevilla

"La Casa de Carlos V" was built within the complex, but is actually a different building and in the Renaissance style.

The Currans in Carlos V's Gardens

"La Plaza de España" and the World's Fair

Mark on the Bridge, "la Plaza de España," Sevilla

Keah and the Tiled Madrid Scene, "la Plaza de Espana"

Pavillions were constructed to imitate the real thing for the fair and festivities of 1929. Bridges, fountains, and beautiful "azulejos" with scenes from all the provinces of Spain were reproduced.

"Las Palomas Blancas," Professor Michael Flys, Sevilla

"Las Palomas Blancas," Katie

Dr. Flys and Katie showed their patience with the "palomitas" of the Plaza María Luisa.

The Flamenco Show, Sevilla

That first evening the entire group went to the "Patio Sevillano" for a live flamenco show, one of two on the trip. It alternated "cante jondo" with regional dances. We sat in a great spot next to the side of the stage. It was a quite a performance; of particular interest to Mark the amateur classic guitar player, the guitarist was excellent with "jazzed up" improvised guitar work matched to the "cante jondo" and the voice of two "gitanos." The guitar starts, the "gitano" warms up, than all match the dancers. There was "Zapateado," etc. Katie had her hair fixed and was all ready for the big show; she loved it; a most entertaining night.

"LA GIRA"—TRAVEL TO CENTRAL, NORTHERN AND NORTHWESTERN SPAIN

We were all up early for the long bus ride. And there were sleepyheads. There was wheat, olive groves, rolling hills, and then we passed through a part of the Sierra Morena (literature students can only think of "Don Quixote de la Mancha") and then the long haul to Mérida. It was barren and dry on the way.

MÉRIDA

We arrived in Mérida about noon, and it was hot as blazes. It was founded in 25 B.C. by Caesar Augustus at the side of the Guadiana River near to the road between Salamanca and Sevilla, and Toledo and Lisbon. It became the "Capital of Lusitania."

The Roman Ruins at Mérida

These then were the Roman ruins. There was a reconstructed theater of the original by Agrippa, a son-in-law of Caesar Augustus in 24 B.C. There was a semi-circle of stone tiers, a pit for the choral players, and a high stage wall with a covered colonnade and statues. (It reminded of what we would see in Ephesus in a later trip, the scene from the library).

Due to the excessive heat we did not do the visit to Cáceres. One should note however that in Cáceres one of the three military orders of Spain - the military Order of Santiago de Calatrava -was founded in 1170 to protect the pilgrims on the way to Santiago de Compostela. We did see from the bus some outstanding mansions of 15th and 16th centuries.

The trip continued through mountains like I would imagine in Bavaria, down into rolling hills of wheat near Salamanca. Upon entering the city we saw the cathedral with a nice view of the Tormes River. We stayed at an old, small hotel near the Plaza Mayor. There were "cigueña" or stork nests on the church towers all over this part of the country. We would spend three days in Salamanca.

June 29th SALAMANCA

The Storks ("Cigueñas") La Plaza de Salamanca

After arriving we had drinks outside the hotel in the Plaza Mayor, listened to music from the "tunas," that is, the students dressed in gowns and faculty ribbons and singing sometimes ribald university songs, and saw the famous storks or "cigueñas" on the steeples; they migrate back and forth from Northern Africa to Salamanca.

Baile Folclórico, Salamanca

The Plaza was also the site of folkloric dances from northern Spain which we were able to see.

The next day we would do intensive tourism in Salamanca: The Plaza Mayor, Casa de las Conchas, La Clerecía Church, la Catedral Vieja and the Catedral Nueva. We then saw the Universidad de Salamanca: "la Sala de Miguel de Unamuno" and "la Sala de Fray Luis de León" (Spain's best Renaissance poet Garcilaso de la Vega was his student) the latter in the Plateresque style.

Socializing in Salamanca

That p.m. we were with friends of the Flys's, Menchita, Nico, Patricia, and Nicky at their home outside of Salamanca. There was swimming in the pool, "paella y vino y coñac." We really had good conversation in Spanish including Mark and Nico's talk of western films in the U.S. cinema. Menchita is the principal of a primary school; she is very "viva" and "ambiciosa." There was good "plática" in the p.m. on Spain and Spanish politics. Mark remembers this as one of the few times where he really experienced and thoroughly enjoyed an intellectual talk in Spanish in Spain!

Katie at the Burger King, Salamanca

Later that evening we were back to Salamanca and a visit to the Burger King! Everyone, all the "gringos" that is, were, as the Brazilians say, "curing their homesickness" with the food.

That night after Keah went early to bed, John Griggs and I went to the Plaza Mayor to see and hear the "Tunas." Keah and I had seen the folk dancing earlier in the day, a nice atmosphere.

On one of the days in Salamanca in the p.m. we returned to Menchita's house, a swim at pool, snacks of potato salad and then seafood: "almejas, gambas, langostinos y cigalas." Then there was a sad goodbye to Katie, a bit hard on all of us. She will stay with Menchita, Nico and the kids while the ASU group does the "gira" to León, Santiago de Compostela, and the NW. We will come and pick her up in Salamanca on July 8th or 9th. Tamara is staying as well, so they will have great fun.

That night it was rainy and cold. The Plaza Mayor was almost empty. I slept like a log for the second straight night in spite of incredible street noise. The students were still out at 4-5 a.m.; their partying was amazing, night after night.

What follows is the background and history of what we saw in wonderful Salamanca.

Salamanca and Its History

It dates from the earliest natives of the Peninsula, "los Iberos" that is. The town was later conquered by Hannibal in the 3rd century B.C. and later flourished under the Romans as evidenced by the bridge across the Tormes. It was invaded several times by the Moors, but was taken by the Christians in the "Reconquista" by Alfonso VI in 1085.

There was feuding among the leading Spanish families in the 14th and 15th centuries.

The University was founded in 1215; one might note that Oxford was in 1167 followed by Bologna. It was part of the patronage of the Kings of Castile and was important in the days of the Counter-Reform in the 16th century.

Salamanca was occupied by the French in 1811 and was freed by the Duke of Wellington in 1812.

Salamanca: the Literary Heritage

The Cathedral, the "Río Tormes" of "Lazarillo de Tormes" Fame and the Stone Bulls

Salamanca is intrinsically involved with the great Spanish literary heritage of the Picaresque novel with "Lazarillo de Tormes," the above picture showing the Tormes River and the ancient stone bulls that played a part in the novel, 1525-1554. The novel lists an anonymous author but is among the best of the small genre in Spain. It treats an anti-hero who must live by his wits to survive, and the structure is with each chapter detailing the adventures of the hero with a different "amo" or boss. I took a course on the "Novela Picaresca" at the National University of Mexico in the early 1960s and made the mistake of asking the learned professor "Which is the best of the novels?" We were to do a long paper on our choice. She said, "Guzmán de Alfarache." So I spent many hours that summer reading a one thousand page novel in 16th century Spanish Prose. I should have chosen "Lazarillo de Tormes" and its perhaps 150 pages. It has much more humor as well. Folks in Literature claim that such novels really depicted an accurate view of the poor class in Spain in the midst of all that gold and riches flowing in from America to the nobility and the upper class.

Also from the Golden Age was the priest-poet Fray Luis de León one of my favorites in Spanish Letters. One only needs to recall the short poem "Vida Retirada" a jewel of early Renaissance verse in Spain when the poet recalls the much used theme of escaping the vicissitudes of life in the Royal Court for a simpler existence in the country. Fray Luis had his own vicissitudes, among them being accused by the ubiquitous Spanish Inquistion for daring to translate the "Song of Songs" from the Old Testament to Spanish. There were veiled accusations that he might actually be Jewish with ancestors who were "conversos" or converts to the faith. He spent some time in their jail but obviously survived and was a major scholar, writer and teacher at the University in the 16th century.

One of Fray Luis's students went on to even greater literary fame than the master. This is Garcilaso de la Vega, Spain's best Renaissance and Golden Age Poet. Using themes from classical Greece and Rome but with a stylized yet very readable Spanish he wrote the famous "Eclogues." I would have an amazing semester seminar on his poetry taught by Dr. Edward Sarmiento, a true master of Spanish, Spanish Literature and Spain and marvelous teacher on the graduate level.

I'll say much more about San Juan de la Cruz and Santa Teresa de Jesus when the "Gira" arrives to Ávila and Segovia, and Spain's great Golden Age Dramatist Calderón de la Barca when we arrive in Madrid. And Miguel de Unamuno when we pass through Alcalá de Henares on the way to the Basque Country.

Tourist Sites in Salamanca

La Plaza Mayor

"La Plaza Mayor," Salamanca

It is three stories all around; the Churriguera brothers did most of it. It was constructed by King Felipe V as thanks for victory in the War of the Spanish Succession.

"La Casa de las Conchas"

The Casa de las Conchas is from the 15th century; there are 400 shells or "conchas" on its sides and it has Isabelline windows (it corresponds to the Manueline Style in Portugal at about the same time).

The University of Salamanca

Patio of the University of Salamanca, the Statue of Fray Luis de León

The University was founded in 1215; one might note once again that Oxford dates from 1167 followed by Bologna. It was part of the patronage of the Kings of Castile and became important in the days of the Counter-Reform in the 16th century. As detailed earlier, it is intrinsically involved with the great Spanish literary heritage of the Picaresque novel with "Lazarillo de Tormes," 1525-1554, the Renaissance-"Mystic" Poet Fray Luis de León, the Mystic San Juan de la Cruz, the Renaissance-Golden Age poet Garcilaso de la Vega, the Golden Age dramatist Calderón de la Barca and the Iconoclastic Philospher-Thinker Unamuno as Rector in the 1930s.

Highlights of the visit to the university were . . .

The Plateresque Entrance and Fray Luis

"El Patio de la Escuela." This is the entrance to the Universidad de Salamanca. It dates from 1534 and was done primarily in the Plateresque style; there are three levels to the entrance, the first from the time of the Reyes Católicos, the second from Carlos V, the third from a Pope. Note the basket handle arches.

The Hapsburg Entrance—the Double Eagle

This entrance is done in the Plateresque style and depicts the Hapsburg Double Eagle.

Unamuno's Examination Bench

The guide book points out that this was the classroom of Miguel de Unamuno, Rector of the University. He was as well a "catedrático" or Full Professor of Greek. A Basque from Bilbao he became Rector of the University in the 1930s and was a staunch liberal and Republican of the times, thus an enemy of Francisco Franco and the Military. We shall say more about him when we arrive in the Basque Country.

Fray Luis's Pulpit

The pulpit from which Fray Luis de León lectured with the student benches with carved student names in front of it. We searched for but we never found Garcilaso de la Vega's. All these figures were important to me during my years of graduate study of Spanish Literature at Saint Louis University and even more when I taught on a regular basis the Survey of Spanish Literature—Golden Age—at Arizona State University. Fray Luis is buried in the Chapel.

The ASU Student Group at the University

A final literary aside: the University of Salamanc was one of the highlights of Spain in relation to my studies of Golden Age Spanish literature; Córdoba and its connection to "El Príncipe de la Escuridad," Luis de Góngora, was a close second. Madrid and writers there in the 17th century followed. I do not know how many students in our group realized this, but for sure the ole' professors did!

Plateresque Entrance of the New Cathedral

Salamanca—the New Cathedral 1513-1560. It is late Gothic and Plateresque, the huge entrance door of sculpted stone, and a Baroque Chapel.

The Old Cathedral and the Skyline of Salamanca

"Retablo" and the High Altar, the Old Cathedral

It is 12th century Romanesque and old Gothic with an outstanding "retablo" or high altar from 1445. The very impressive apse with its many compartments was painted in 1445-1453.

The Exam Seat, Professor Mark, the Santa Bárbara Chapel

The cathedral has a famous chapel; the Santa Bárbara Chapel was the selected place for university exams. The candidate sits with feet on the Bishop's tomb and his cold, stone feet and prays for guidance. The ole' professor had to take his place as those suffering students did in the old days and was reminded of the three days of written exams for the Ph.D. at Saint Louis University. I might have gotten cold feet in Salamanca.

The Eleventh Century Romanesque Church of San Marcos

The Church of San Marcos

Keah and I discovered this amazing place on a "paseo" after the official tour. We had walked past the Plaza Mayor, back to the Cathedral, to the University, and then came upon the "Iglesia de San Marcos." The latter was really unusual for us; it was from the 1100s, was round in shape with narrow slits for windows in the thick medieval walls, and was "Mozárabic" inside. It seemed to be the epitome of the medieval walled-fortress church.

SANTIAGO DE COMPOSTELA

"La Gira" continues: on the road to Santiago de Compostela in Galicia

We began the bus trip to Santiago de Compostela, passing through Zamora. They still have stone fences along wheat fields. Later the countryside became a bit bleak with rolling hills and the hand cutting of the grass or hay in the fields. There was a nice stream and they say it is trout fishing country. But the last thirty kilometers into Santiago reminded of Portugal; all was green and the vineyards were everywhere along the road. And oxen carts accompanied the cars and buses.

History and Highlights of Santiago de Compostela

It is a city and region based upon legend. St. James or "Santiago el Mayor," was believed to be the apostle of Jesus who eventually would Christianize Spain. After the death of Jesus he leaves Judea and arrives in the Iberian Peninsula. During a period of seven years he seems to have little success in converting the Iberians to Christianity, but then the Virgin Mary appears to him in Zaragoza, thus initiating the legend of the "Virgin del Pilar." He then begins to convert many people. Eventually he goes back to Judea and is killed by Herod. His disciples bring the body back to Spain to be enterred. The grave is lost until the 9th century when a star leads shepherds to it. In 844 A.D. King Don Ramiro I is battling the Moors at Clavijo, near Logroño. A knight on horseback with sword in hand appears, a red cross on his banner, and with his help the Spanish defeat the Moors. The knight was believed to be the apostle! As a result St. James the Apostle becomes the patron saint of the "Reconquista"—St. James the Moor Killer or "Santiago Matamoros."

When the relics of St. James were discovered in the 9th century a cult arose. Its fame grew over all Europe and Santiago de Compostela in the 11th century became ranked with Rome and Jerusalem as one of three major Christian Pilgrimage sites or "peregrinajes cristianas." At this time the Turks controlled the eastern Mediterranean, so with that limitation in travel to Jerusalem, Santiago in what would become Spain becomes even more popular. At around this time the French united with the Spaniards and were involved with a great battle with the Moors. French, Germans, English and even Scandinavianas begin to make the pilgrimage to Santiago. Cities like León along the way to Santiago become famous.

The Monastery of Compostela was originally administered and controlled by the Benedictine and Cistercian monks and was protected by the Knights Templar—the "Orden de la Espada Roja." The costume or clothing of the pilgrims became a tradition: a cape, a staff, sandals and a broad brimmed hat with scallop shells on the hat, this in 1130 A.D. The "Pilgrims' Guide" or "Guía de Peregrinajes" at the Cathedral makes a big thing of all this. Important as well for the modern pilgrim is the "Pilgrim's Passport" which must be stamped in France at the beginning of the long trip to Santiago, in inns along the way and finally at the office of the church in Santiago. A plenary Indulgence may be granted along with the completed passport!

In medieval times there were at one time some 500,000 to two million pilgrims per year, then came a gradual decline because of assault and thievery of the pilgrims along the pilgrims' route and wars between Christian countries.

The English Corsair Sir Francis Drake armed with instructions from Queen Elizabeth to "singe the beard of Felipe II the Spanish King" attacked nearby Coruña in 1589. The local bishop hid the relics of Santiago for fear of further attacks; they were then lost for 300 years during which the pilgrimage was abandoned.

The relics were rediscovered in 1879 and were recognized by the Pope as legitimate, so pilgrimages started again. Plenary indulgences were given with visits during a holy year.

There were two ways to get there—via Asturias which was dangerous and the "Vía Francesa."

The Cathedral-Basilica was built on the site of the tomb. It was destroyed by the Moor Al Mansur in 997. The current Basilica dates from 11th, 12th, and 13th centuries. In 1386 John of Gaunt crowned himself King of Castile and León in the cathedral.

Tourist Highlights of Santiago de Compostela:

The "Obradeiro" Façade, Santiago de Compostela

The "Obradeiro" Façade which is a baroque masterpiece was done in 1750. Behind the façade is the original cathedral of the Romanesque age.

"El Pórtico de la Gloria," 1

"El Pórtico de la Gloria," 2

The "Pórtico de la Gloria" in the old cathedral is the oldest carving in the entire edifice; it is 12th century Romanesque, considered the best stone carving of medieval times in Spain. The guidebooks emphasize the personality of the figures carved and the belief and or superstition that one received good luck or a blessing by placing the imprint of the five fingers of the right hand in the proper place on the pillar before entering the church.

The "Botafumeiro" unfortunately not shown here, a huge incense boat, is used on special occasions. For years I showed a documentary film in SPA 473, Civilization of Spain, of the mass at Santiago de Compostela with the brotherhood in action in the swinging of the huge boat. It is from two to three meters high, with an appearance like an old pot bellied stove; it is attached to a very heavy rope from the ceiling above the altar and is swung back and forth at given times before, during and after mass by two or three brothers who control it with other ropes. The boat swings like a pendulum in almost the entirety of the transept of the huge church. It is finally slowed and stopped by a brother literally with a bear hug. The saying is that the incense was needed to fill the church thus hiding the stench of all those dirty, sweaty pilgrims in attendance.

The Golden Baroque High Altar, the Church of Santiago de Compostela

The high altar in the center with its 13th century statue of Santiago the Apostle is sumptuous and some say "gaudy" in appearance. It was completed in true Baroque style and splendor in the 16th century. Some say it all is a "baroque monstrosity." One can go through a small corridor behind the main altar and touch (or kiss) the mantle of the image of the saint. Under the altar is a tomb constructed with the remains of the 9th century church; it is believed to contain the bones of the saint himself.

Tourism and Socializing in Santiago de Compostela

On the first night in Santiago de Compostela we went to the Plaza de España with the huge cathedral, the "ayuntamiento," and the Hotel - Parador. There were drinks of "Ribeiro Claro," like the "vinho verde de Portugal," and "caldo galego" at "Fornas" Restaurant.

Entryway, "Parador Fernando I," Old "Hospital de los Reyes"

The next a.m. was the official tour. Afterwards Keah and I investigated the great national "Parador," the "Rey Fernando."

With the "Tunas" in Santiago de Compostela Plaza

There was a chance encounter with the now familiar "tunas" or student musical groups throughout much of Spain. The long black academic robes and accompanied ribbons were impressive. They offered cassete tapes of their recordings for sale.

With the Group for Dinner, Santiago de Compostela

The Party with the "Tunas," Santiago de Compostela

That night was a time of a big party or "noche de parranda" with a big crowd. There was "Vino Ribeiro, caldo gallego, y pimiento," singing with the "tunas," the students from Navarra, and the party continued with students in the hotel. The next day all felt a bit for the worse.

There had been mass in the Cathedral in the earlier p.m. with Miguel, Felisa, Mike, Sharon, John Griggs, Tim, and Keah. That was when we saw the aforementioned huge incense boat or "bota fumeiro."

PONTEVEDRA AND "LAS RÍAS"

Using Santiago as a staging point the next a.m. the group did a two hour bus ride to Pontevedra. Keah and I loved it; it was like northern Portugal. We saw the "horreos" (stone granaries of Galicia) with "carros de bueyes y viñas," stone crosses in each village, and terrain similar to that around Guimarães in Portugal. There were women working in the fields, ladies all dressed in black.

Then we arrived at Pontevedra and the "Rias" or Fiords. It was absolutely gorgeous, but all seemed a blur because we passed through this area so quickly. We saw beautiful beaches along the coast which is a vacation spot in hot August for the Madrileños.

We crossed the bridge to the Dorna Restaurant for a "Gallego" lunch of "sopa de mariscos" with a bit of everything including crab and "gambas a la plancha." There was a view of the "ria" and photos of persons fishing from the bridge. They would dig, pull, and dredge the bottom for clams or "almejas." We all felt the frustration of seeing gorgeous beaches on the way home and not able to stop. I wrote: "I would love to come back here and check things out. The countryside is beautiful - the "Rias" and the ocean at Pontevedra."

The Market in Santiago de Compostela

Then the bus headed back to Compostela for a "free day" of doing laundry and a visit to the market which had wonderful fruit including good peaches and chickens. We did our last walk to Cathedral Square and then repaired to the "regular" bar for "Ribeiro" and "tapas." There we were joined by Josie, Katie, Florence, Mike and Sharon, and John for "caldo gallego." There was some good "tuna" music and home to bed.

LEÓN

July 4[th.] The bus continues to León. It was green and pretty until Orense, then rougher country. Galicia in retrospect really agreed with me. We checked into the Hotel Paris in León.

León was a medieval city, the capital of Asturias in the 10th century, with walls surrounding the city built on top of Roman ruins. The Kings of Asturias populated León with "Mozárabe" people (Christian refugees from Córdoba and Toledo), thus in the 11th and 12th centuries León became the center of "Mozarabic Spain." It has the entire gamut of architectural styles: the Romanesque (San Isidoro), the Gothic (the Cathedral) and the Renaissance (San Marcos). It became a major stop on the "Way of Santiago."

Tourism in León. July 5th

The Cathedral

Stained Glass, the Cathedral, León

Originally a masterpiece of the Gothic in the 13th century and completed only in the 16th, there was a baroque choir, but the real feature is the stained glass, almost 1800 square meters of the same, 125 windows and 57 "oculi," dating from the 13th to the 15th centuries, comparable to Rheims, Chartres and the best of French Gothic. No other church in Spain can match this. The Cathedral is one of three on the "Way of St. James" along with Burgos and the Cathedral of Santiago de Compostela itself. It is one of the outstanding churches of all Spain.

"Retablo," the Cathedral, León

The Church of San Isidoro

Entrance, San Isidoro Church, León

Close Up, Entrance, San Isidoro, the Knight Santiago Matamoros

It represented the best of the Romanesque with rounded arches and paintings in the original 12th century style; I found the paintings a bit reminiscent of the "Casa del Marqués" in Tunja, Colombia, although Tunja was centuries later and it is probably more coincidence than based on art. We saw the medieval manuscripts "illuminated" by the monks. The church has an amazing history: it was done on the site of an ancient Roman temple. It was constructed and dedicated in 1063 to the memory of St. Isidoro of Seville, archbishop and Doctor of the Church in Visigothic Spain and prior to the Moorish invasions. His cadaver was brought to Leon for veneration since Sevilla was now in the hands of the Moors. Little remains of the original church; the remains now are of the 12th century. In the Royal Pantheon of the Kings of Asturias one sees "los capitales," pillars and arches, the first in Spain to be decorated with frescos. The tombs of the Kings are done in Romanesque art with 12th century murals in a fine state of preservation. I really felt that here we saw medieval Spain!

Monastery and Church of San Marcos

It was associated with the Knights of the Order of Santiago since the 12th century, the home base of the soldier-monks who protetected the pilgrims on the way to Santiago. Three centuries later Ferdinando el Católico, the "Gran Maestro de Santiago," maintained the church as a central place for the order and its riches garnered in the conquest of Spain. The church and monastery were finished by Carlos V in Renaissance style.

The "Parador" of León to the Side of San Marcos

The "parador" to the side was replete with armor, a nice cloister with Roman ruins, antique furniture of 16th and 17th centuries and many paintings. It was $150 US per night in 1987 and had the feeling of a real palace and monastery with three or four floors wrapping around a quadrangle. The façade finished in the 18th century has medallions which depict biblical figures and the shell theme of the pilgrims to Santiago as well as figures from Rome and Spain. The main doorway has a representation of the life of Santiago.

The Hallway inside the "Parador"

Wall Scene of Santiago Matamoros, León

Keah, Interior Patio of the "Parador"

"Portada" of the "Parador," "Santiago el Apóstolo"

There was a nice lunch near the Hotel Paris with local wine, a "clarete" for 200 pesetas per bottle. We drank (some of us) a great deal of it and Mark and John returned to the Cathedral for our "juerga." Mark was singing and whistling ersatz Gregorian chant in that incredibly large church filled with echos before we were both thrown out by the sacristan. There was repentance and remorse the next a.m.

After León we began the trip south eventually heading to Madrid. An eventful stop was at the old capital of Valladolid and its famous castle of Simancos. The Castle of Simancos is now a national archive. Valladolid's heyday was in medieval Spain. It was settled in pre-Roman times by the Celts and later the Romans. It was controlled by the Moors in the 8th century. But it became important in the Middle Age as the seat of the Court of Castile. The Catholic Kings Isabel I of Castile and Ferdinand II of Aragon married in Valladolid in 1469 and established it as the capital of the Kingdom of Castile and of a united Spain. Christopher Columbus died there in 1506 and writers Quevedo and Cervantes lived and worked in the city. But after a fire in the castle Felipe II moved the capital to Madrid. The castle was a grey stone edifice but seemed cold and a bit forboding compared to its counterparts in Sintra or Óbidos in Portugal; it had been used principally as a prison by the grandees of Spain. The Spanish Literature major can only think of poor Segismundo in Calderón de la Barca's "La Vida Es Sueño." "Qué is la vida? Un frenesí! Una illusion! Un sueño! Y los sueños sueños son!"

ÁVILA

Mark in Front of the Wall of Ávila

At an altitude of 3710 feet it is the highest provincial capital in all Spain with the extremes of climate of the "meseta española," extreme cold in winter and tremendous heat in summer. It was called "Ávila de los Caballeros," founded together with Segovia and Salamanca by King Alfonso VI in 1085 after the conquest of Toledo as part of a second line of defense to the south of the Duero River. The Knights of Ávila were instrumental in the retaking of Zaragoza in the 12th century and Córdoba, Jaén and Sevilla in the 13th. It reached its peak in the 15th century but many of its nobles left for Toledo in the 16th century when Carlos V established his court there.

Keah, Flowers and the Wall of Ávila

The walled medieval city is most famous in literary circles due to Santa Teresa de Jesus, 1515-1588, mystic and Doctor of the Church, and San Juan de la Cruz, 1542-1591, her spiritual counselor and partner. Santa Teresa founded the "Carmelitas Descalzas" and their many convents and monasteries. She was joined by San Juan who worked doing the same for the monks. Both became known as mystics of the Spanish Catholic Church, but a clarification may be in order. If by "mystic" one means the experience of being at least briefly united with God in this life in some way through prayer, meditation and the like, they qualify. See Santa Teresa's "Las Moradas" and San Juan's "Noche Oscura del Alma." Both are held as major figures in what we can call the Counter-Reform in Spain, that amazing effort in the 16th and 17th centuries to defend the Catholic Church from the rise of Protestantism in Europe. One also cannot discount the role of the Jesuits in the Council of Trent in 1541 as well in defending the Pope, the Church, and the role of action along with faith for the salvation of man's soul.

The medieval city walls were impressive enough, perfectly surrounding the town, but inside the town itself my notes said it all seemed cold, worn, and sandy brown with little sense of its being preserved (once again it seemed night and day compared to Óbidos). The cathedral was done with lines of rounded stones.

The weather was memorable: me in walking shorts and with a cold, wet wind.

The Church-Basilica of Santa Teresa de Jesus, Ávila

The House of Santa Teresa de Jesus

It is now a church with several convents nearby (recalling her role along with St. John of the Cross in founding convents for the "Carmelitas Descalzas.") One of the relics caught my attention: her ring finger with an emerald ring and bones of St. John of the Cross.

The ASU Group in Front of the Walled City of Ávila

MADRID PART I

Our arrival in Madrid—the second phase of teaching and travel in Spain

History and Literary History

The site was originally a small town until the Moors built a fortress they called "Majerit." The fortress was captured by Alfonso VI in 1083. The city was dedicated to the "Virgen de la Almudena" due a statue found nearby of her. The Spanish kings came to the site from the 14th century on and the Catholic Kings came in 1477 to inaugurate the Monastery of "San Jerónimo el Real." Carlos V later reconstructed the old Moorish fortress of el Alcázar. It was decreed to be the capital of Spain in 1561 in place of Valladolid and later Toledo, this by King Felipe II. But only in the 18th century did serious construction of buildings like the Palacio Real begin.

In literary terms once again this is the city of several major figures of Golden Age Spanish Literature, among them Lope de Vega, 1562-1635. Born in Madrid, Lope studied with the Jesuits at Alcalá de Henares, participated in the "Armada Invencible" against the English and King Henry VIII in 1588, and lived at Toledo and Madrid, life in the court. Called "el Monstruo de a Naturaleza" by no less than Cervantes for his vast work, reputed to be perhaps 1800 plays (about 500 are extant) he was the outstanding playwright of all Spain. His life was a drama in itself with many marriages, more dalliances, a brief vocation as priest and adventures as well and then a return to court life. Of most significance was that he was a commoner but without doubt a true genius in the complete sense of the word.

Secondly, it was the center of activity of the great dramatist Pedro Calderón de la Barca 1600-1681. After a swashbuckling life as soldier and then the priesthood and studies with the Jesuits and then Salamanca he was named Dramatist of the Court. Calderón in a sense was the opposite of Lope and after continuing Lope's development of the Baroque Spanish drama (as in "La Vida es Sueño") he dedicated the final part of his life to sacred plays, the "Autos Sacramentales."

Two hundred years later one of Madrid's main writers would be José Zorilla 1817-1893, Romantic poet and author of "Don Juan Tenorio." (One might recall that there was a Golden Age Don Juan by a cleric—Tirso de Molina - in that one the hero is indeed sent to the fires of hell without repentance as opposed to the Romantic's solution of salvation through his heroine.) And then came the great prose writers of 19th century, the liberal Pérez Galdós and others.

Life in Madrid

Madrid, the Dorm of the "Colegio Mayor de Alcalá"

We arrived at the college dorm, our residence for the coming weeks. It seemed old and a bit worn but pleasant enough. It was called the "Colegio Mayor Alcalá." We were in a bit of a state of shock over "dorm" life, the tiny rooms, and noise, loud rock music at that. Madrid was cool and rainy when we arrived, unusual they said for that time of year. That would change soon enough. Many student groups are housed here including the summer programs of the Universities of Alabama and Tennesse, so it was crowded.

Keah and Katie cannot operate on the street without me, so I am feeling some pressure. We were facing a huge city, laundry needing to be done, passport and travel arrangements, etc. plus an awkward situation with classes and tutoring. I said it would a long month here unless things change for the better. Fortunately they did.

The lounge at the Colegio Mayor was run by Jacinto and it consisted in a bar-café. There was good, reasonably priced food and beer. It became the focal point of all our social life—students and faculty. Jacinto was a lifesaver!

Katie, Statues of Don Quixote, "Rocinante el Caballo" and
Sancho Panza, La Plaza de España, Madrid

There was no separate dormitory room available for Katie and Tamara yet. Keah and I took off on a circular bus to the Plaza de España and to Meliá Tourism to try to arrange the trip to France and to Lourdes. It coincides with the travel rush of all Europeans on vacation in August. We shall see.

"La Gran Vía," Madrid

The Symbol of Madrid, "el Oso"

"La Plaza Mayor de Madrid," King Felipe III

We then continued in downtown Madrid walking on the "Gran Vía" with its souvenir shops, to "Calle del Carmen, Galerias Preciadas, y Corte Inglés," a lunch on Carmen, and then a walk to the Plaza Mayor. It dates from the 16th century with King Felipe III's statue in the middle, and it seemed grungy in the daytime. We encountered surly shoe shiners and waiters and inflated prices at the "Arco de Cuchilleros."

We walked on "Calle del Jerónimo," went to a fine guitar shop (more on that later), then checking out the Palace Hotel, the famous "Plaza de Cibeles" and home. Our metro connections were "Sol, Cuatro Caminos y Metropolitana, Linea n. 6." There was beer and dinner in Jacinto's bar and talk with students later back at the dorm.

Then we began the first classes in Madrid; I had Joe in the "Don Quixote" and the tutorial with Lori for the second year grammar review. Lunch was at the school. Katie is now home from Salamanca. We went shopping with Katie on the "Gran Vía"—the weather was hot, but we stopped at Burger King for cold ice cream!

"La Plaza de Cristóbal Colón"

On another morning we took the subway to the Plaza Colón, to TWA Security with John and Mike, then a humongous walk to the French Embassy at "Nuevos Ministerios" (for the visa to France for the Lourdes trip). We were exhausted, sweaty and hot. Then we took the subway home.

That afternoon Keah, Katie and I went back to the Plaza Colón via subway to TWA; we are all set with boarding passes to Phoenix on August 5th. It seemed very smooth and efficient.

After TWA we went past the National Library with statues of Cervantes, Luis Vives, Lope de Vega and inside there were paintings of Luis de Góngora, Lope, and others.

The Triumphal Arch of King Carlos III

"Avenida Castellanas," Madrid

There were views of the Triumphal Arch of King Carlos III imitating all the predecessors including the Emperors of Rome and the later "Arc de Triomphe," then "Avenida Castellanas." Eventually the long outing continued down to the "Plaza de Cibeles." The big "Edificio de Comunicaciones" (the post office) was in view. Then the "Plaza de la Independencia" (1778) with its statue of Carlos III, then to the "Parque del Buen Retiro."

THE "CORRIDA DE TOROS" OR BULL FIGHT AT LAS VENTAS ARENA

I called it "the bull fight of the century" in dripping sarcasm, meaning the worst! The most memorable moment was the "corre corre" and masses crowding out of the arena when it was over and jamming into the Metro where one of our students, one of the adults, had her purse sliced and valuables stolen. I still believe I may have been staring the thief in the face during the crowded ride but was aware of nothing. Those guys were good! Strangely enough I have no notes as to the bull fight itself nor the music, so it must not have made much of an impression. But Las Ventas is the most famous arena in all Spain.

We received our "carnet" or student pass so we were off and running to monuments and museums in Madrid. The pass to the Prado Museum would be well used.

July 11 to 17th Life in Madrid

There is no practical way here to document the daily life and many days and things in Madrid but the following list gives an idea:

The "Torre de España," the "circular" bus, the dolphins' fountain with its geese

The Prado. An early and initial visit was to see the Flemish Rooms (Rubens, Titian).

The Gaidiano Museum

Chinese restaurants

Shopping—"El Corte Inglés"

Retiro Park—the Lake

The Archeological Museum: it was immense and overwhelming. There were the salons of Pre-History, Greek, Roman, Egyptian, Iberian, Visigoth, Moorish Conquest and on up to the 15th century.

The Ritz Hotel

The "Zarzuela" "La Verbena de la Paloma"

The Park along Castellanas, Recoletos

The list at least indicates what I cannot document here. More follows.

Entrance to "Las Cuevas" and Famous "Tapas," Madrid

After an exhausting day of sightseeing to the park around the "Plaza de España," to the "Palacio Real," to the plaza by the "Plaza Mayor," we ended up in the famous "las cuevas" and its "mesones" where we saw Miguel, Felisa, Mike, Sharon and John and experimented all kinds of Spain's "tapas" at their source! In the plaza outside we heard classical guitar music and there was a caricature artist who did Katie. The evening ending with a short visit to McDonald's for some very good ice cream and home on the "metro," exhausted.

Mark and Keah, the Fountain and Entry to "El Parque del Buen Retiro"

The Students, the Lake and the "Monumento del Buen Retiro"

The Park belonged to the Spanish monarchy until the nineteenth century when it became a public place. Centrally located it was handy to the "Puerta de Alcalá" (the entrance to the "Plaza Mayor") and the Prado Museum. It has been the center of city life since the Hapsburgs when famous Golden Age Plays were performed. The Count-Duke of Olivares whose painting we shall see shortly gave additional plots of land to the kings to build palaces and such. Ups and downs including damage by Napoleon's troops in the 19th century are also part of its history. But it remains today as a beautiful green gathering place in a huge metropolitan area.

These photos feature our outing to the "Parque del Buen Retiro," and rowing on the lake with one of my favorite students Ana Maria. There were later drinks at a café near the Parque and a view of city traffic and the "Correos." That night there were Pakistani dances and music in the Colegio Mayor.

First Visit to the Prado Art Museum

Entrance to El Prado Art Museum

I was overwhelmed by what I saw; I could not believe that there were entire rooms full of El Greco, Velásquez, and many rooms of Goya! And this was not to mention Egyptian, Roman, and Italian Renaissance art by the masters. It was a kind of Spanish professor's dream comes true. The following are my comments and notes from the various visits. The photos that follow are from the website of the Metropolitan Museum of Art in New York used with written permission. The reason for them is that the Prado did not allow photos and the commercial slides are copyrighted. It is better to see samples of El Greco and Velázquez than none at all. The reader today can simply "Google" the Prado and see all that we saw during those weeks in Madrid, but I think my notes might be a bit helpful and add perspective to the experience.

The Flemish Room - Rubens' imitation of Titiano was amazing.

Berrenguete's "Auto Da Fe" is important simply for depicting the reality of the Spanish Inquisition.

There are dozens of paintings by El Greco, Diego de Velázquez, Goya and then Pablo Picasso in the Annex.

Lladró statue of El Greco, Curran's Souvenirs

These are my notes from lectures on El Greco; one sees there was much speculation!

One sees in the hands his "manierismo." Someone said the small human heads were done intentionally to indicate "a less human brain and more dependence upon God." The muted colors and stormy skies were perhaps indicative of his troubles with the Inquisition for his free use and shifting of Biblical stories: ex. "Las Tres Marías" and the "Descent of the Holy Spirit upon the Apostles." There are two levels in many of his paintings: man and God, earth and heaven. ("El Entierro del Conde Orgaz" is one of them). The "luminosity" and "tearful eyes" are a sign of religiosity and perhaps "from insane asylum models" dependent only on God. Example: the "Cristo Crucificado" or the "Anunciación":

Christ Carrying the Cross. El Greco (Domenikos Theotokopoulos) (Greek, Iráklion (Candia) 1540/41 – 1614 Toledo). Bequest of George Blumenthal, 1941. 41.190.17. Image copyrighted by the Metropolitan Museum of Art.

The Adoration of the Shepherds. El Greco (Domenikos Theotokopoulos) (Greek, Iráklion (Candia) 1540/41 – 1614 Toledo). Bequest of George Blumenthal, 1941. 41.190,17. Image copyrighted by the Metropolitan Museum of Art.

Cardinal Fernando Niño de Guevara (1541 – Domenikos Theotokopoulos) (Greek, Iráklion (Candia) 1540/41 – 1614 Toledo). H.O. Havemeyer Collection, Bequst of Mrs. H.O Havemeyer, 1929. 29.100.5. Image copyrighted by the Metropolitan Museum of Art.

Curran's notes on the paintings of Diego Velázquez:

Velásquez supposedly said, "I can paint only what I see;" therefore there are few religious scenes or themes in his works and there is a stark Spanish Realism replete with subjects from common Spanish people like the "clowns" or "bufones." But of the religious subjects, one is famous: one of his most famous paintings is the "Cristo de Velásquez" which heavily influenced Miguel de Unamuno in the 20th century.

Here are notes from the various paintings:

Velásquez used Greek and pagan themes, for example, Apollo (of the Renaissance) next to a Spanish realist Vulcan. Another example is showing a Mars as a very real person physically.

"Las Hilanderas" or "The Weavers:" this is realism juxtaposed to a pagan theme.

Bacchus and the Spanish Realist "borrrachos" or "drunks." All this is in contrast to a Rubens and his fat, sensual, cherubic pagan scenes.

Velázquez also painted Spain and the empire's history. An example was "Las Lanzas."

"Las Meninas"

Velásquez is painting HIMSELF painting others, in this case the "Infanta" and her maids, but also a mastiff and a dwarf. It is a painting within a painting. The King and Queen are seen in a mirror in the rear of the painting well behind the painter; they are looking on, but they are not the subjects of the painting. Light comes from the right window, the rear window and hallway. Probably more ink has been spilled about this painting than any other in Spain! Most consider it to be Velázquez's masterpiece. I have heard many experts "wax eloquent" going on and on about it. I still remember Mexican intellectual and writer Carlos Fuentes going on about the painting in his series "The Smoking Mirror."

It was while looking at such masterpieces with the entire ASU group looking on and listening to short lectures on the individual pieces that Professor John Griggs and I, in the back of the group, distinctly heard one of the pretty coeds say to her friend, "I hate this shit." We later howled with laughter and anytime thereafter on the trip when we saw something of beauty or intellectual or historic value, John and I would trade quips, saying, "I hate this shit."

The following are examples of the greatness of Velázquez from Mark's photos from galleries in the United States.

Philip IV (1605-1665), King of Spain. Velázquez (Diego Rodríguez de Silva y Velázquez) (Spanish, Seville 1599 – 1660 Madrid). Bequest of Benjamin Altman, 1913. 14.40.639. Image copyrighted by the Metropolitian Museum of Art.

Don Gaspar de Guzmán (1587-1645), Count-Duke of Olivares.
Velázquez (Diego Rodríguez de Silva y Velázquez (Spanish, Seville, 1599 – 1660 Madrid).
Fletcher Fund, 1952. 52. 125. Image copyrighted by the Metropolitan Museum of Art.

Juan de Pareja (born about 1610, Diego Rodríguez de Silva y Velázquez (Spanish, Seville, 1599 – 1660 Madrid). Purchase, Fletcher and Rogers Funds, and Bequest of Miss Adelaide Milton de Groot (1876 – 1967), by exchange, supplemented by gifts from the Museum, 1971. 1971.86. Image copyrighted by the Metropolitan Museum of Art.

"GIRA" TO TOLEDO

View of Toledo. El Greco (Domenikos Theotokopoulos) (Greek, Iráklion (Candia)1540/41 – 1614 Toledo). H. O. Havemeyer Collection, Bequest of Mrs. H. O. Havemeyer, 1929. 29.100.6. Image copyrighted by the Metropolitan Museum of Art.

History and Importance of Toledo

Toledo was founded by the Romans with the Latin name "Toletum" and became the center of the peninsula. After the fall of Rome it passed to the Visigoths who made it their capital and then abandoned it when the Moors attacked and took over in 711 and incorporated Toledo into the emirate of Córdoba. It would remain with this title until 1012 with the revolt of the Taifas and it was elevated to a new status: capital of an independent Taifa kingdom. It was finally retaken in 1085 by Spanish King Alfonso VI of Castile who two years later moved the Spanish capital from León to Toledo and it had the title "Imperial City."

It was the most important city in all Spain for the Jews who reached a population of 12,000 in the 12th century. Alfono X "El Sabio" established the "School of Translators" in Toledo with Jewish participation which lasted until the pogrom in 1355 by the Trastamara family. There was a later massacre and the final straw was the expulsion of the Jews from Spain in 1492. Prior to that Toledo was known in the Middle Age as a place tolerant to the three cultures of the peninsula: Christian, Jewish and Moslem.

The cathedral was begun in 1227 by the Saint King—Ferdinand III.

The "Reyes Católicos" Ferdinando and Isabella of the 15th century liked the city and planned to be buried here—there was a change in plans and they ended in Granada.

Now in the 16th century in 1516 Cardinal Cisneros takes over when Ferdinand dies. Carlos I (Carlos V of Spain) arrives in 1517. Covarrubias at this time was building the "Alcázar."

Toledo received the title of "ciudad" and became the seat of the Spanish Empire in the 1530s.

In 1561 Carlos V's son Felipe II decides to move the court to Madrid.

In 1577 El Greco moves to Toledo.

In the 19th century there is decadence in Toledo when Napoleón Bonaparte occupies the city with his troops; there are fires in San Juan de los Reyes and in the Alcázar.

In 1936 there is the siege of Toledo by the Rebels under Generalísimo Francisco Franco and the Falange.

Toledo today is still the seat of the Cardinal Primate of Spain

Travel and Tourism

View of Toledo

We were quickly out of Madrid on the four-lane and soon saw brown rolling hills and wheat. The first view of Toledo is exciting with the view of the Alcázar and the Cathedral. Our bus followed the road up to the site where El Greco painted it. From there one could see the famous "puertas" or entrances to the city. Amidst all the tourism to be seen, we did see really fine artists doing the "damascene" work—inlay of gold wire on an oxidized steel base.

Bisagra Bridge, Toledo

From el Greco's "View of Toledo" we also saw the Alcázar and then Arab construction in 1000 A.D., then the San Martín Bridge, then "La Puerta de Bisagra." All of Toledo in those days was a walled, fortified city. There are perhaps one half dozen original entryways to the city. One old restored castle outside the walls was governed by El Cid at one time.

THE ALCÁZAR

The "Alcázar," Toledo

It dates from the 13th century and was governed first by El Cid and reconstructed from the 16th century under Carlos V in 1537. It was set afire by the English and the Portuguese in the 17th century in 1710 in the War of the Spanish Succession (the former supported Archduke Carlos of Austria and lost). It was made into a house of charity, then a military academy. As such it suffered the siege by Franco in the Spanish Civil War in 1936.

THE CATHEDRAL

The Cathedral and Entrance, Toledo

Close up, the Cathedral entrance

This is the official Apostolic See of Spain yet today; it is one of the great buildings of Spain. It was built on the site of a Visigoth Cathedral and made a mosque by the Arabs in 1000. After the Spanish took Toledo there was construction in 1227 by King Ferdinando el Santo. The nave was roofed only in 1493; it took 266 years to finish!

Important aspects of the Cathedral

Photos were prohibited and purchased slides are copyrighted. So once again, please "Google" the topic to see all these marvelous scenes.

The portal of 1337

The bell tower, "la gorda," a bell of seventeen and one-half tons cast in 1755

The interior: there are 5 aisles, and it is second in size to that of the Cathedral of Sevilla.

There are 70 stained glass windows in the choir or "coro" in the center of the nave. The largest is the "Rosetón."

The "Reja Renacentista" before the Altar Mayor

The "Retablo Mayor" was done by the Architect Egas for Cardinal Cisneros between 1497 and 1504, "de madera pintada de oro y policromado."

The carved wood choir and seats and double eagle music stand, German from 1646. The lower seats, fifty of them in all, at the end of the "coro" detail 15th century scenes of battle in Granada. The upper part of the choir with seventy seats was carved by Berreguete in the 16th century.

Scenes from the Royal Chapel:

A statue of "Nuestra Señora La Blanca," a smiling virgin, Gothic from the 14th century

El Transparente: the opening in the roof for light for the Cathedral. The windows were opened in the 18th century. The Baroque architects wanted light onto the main altar for showing the Host. The light shines onto what is called the "Altar del Transparente."

The "Sala Capitular" done for Cardinal Cisneros in 1508

In the ante-room there is a "techo mudéjar" from 1508 with "mudéjar" stucco on the entryway. And inside there is a gold leaf ceiling of 1508, still well preserved.

There are portraits of the bishops, the arch-bishop and Cardinals of Toledo, one done by Goya.

The Sacristry:

It is replete with paintings by El Greco.

The Treasury or "El Tesoro:"

The highlight is the Monstrance commissioned by Cardinal Cisneros and done by the artist Enrique de Arce, 1517-1524. They used 37 kilos of gold and it all was the property of Isabella la Católica. There is a newer monstrance from 1594 of 350 pounds of silver with 5,600 pieces, covered with gold—"an offer to the divinity that we most esteem." The gold base is from the 18th century and is Baroque: four angels carry the Holy Sacrament on Corpus Christi.

Other sites in Toledo

El Entierro del Señor de Orgaz. Attributed to Jorge Manuel Theotocópuli (1578 – 1631) After El Greco (1541 -1614) A Photographic Reproduction of a two dimensional public domain work of art. Wikimedia Commons, the free media repository.

"Casa-Museo de El Greco"

This house and museum were inaugurated in 1910 and remain one of the main places to see the great painter's works, although we saw many more in El Prado. El Greco, from Crete, trained by the masters in Rome in the "Manierista" style of course became one of a handful of great painters of Spain's Golden Age. The most famous painting in the "casa-museo" is his "View of Toledo," although there are other copies of it in diverse places. But it was special to see finally the great painting after our initial stop high on the hill overlooking Toledo and seeing the city as he must have as well! The other is the "El Entierro del Conde Orgaz."

"LA SINAGOGA DE SANTA MARÍA LA BLANCA"

"La Sinagoga de Santa María la Blanca"

1357-1360. The Synagogue was done by Samuel ha-Levi, treasurer of the King of Castile Pedro el Cruel. The hall is "Mudéjar" style with 54 arches with marble columns. The Torah was kept in the arches. There is praise of Pedro who protected and favored the Jews during his reign. After the expulsion of the Jews in 1492, in 1494 the building was turned over to the military "Órden de Calatrava" and was used as an oratory to St. Benedict.

"La Sinagoga del Tránsito"

"San Juan de los Reyes" Monastery and Cloister

Interior pátio, San Juan de Reyes Monastery

Interior Patio with Gargoyles, San Juan de los Reyes

The edifice was built by the Spanish after they defeated the Portuguese at Toro and was done at the command of Queen Isabella la Católica herself! The Reyes Católicos had planned to be buried here—thus its elegance—but were enterred later in Granada. It was to be modeled on the Church of San Isidoro in León. It was done in the style of the Gothic-Isabelline and is considered to be the finest building done in Spain by the Catholic Kings! Cardinal Cisneros did his novitiate here. We were interested especially by the gargoyles in the cloister, fine examples of the thinking of the time.

Toledo Crafts

The "Damasceno" Craftsman at Work, Toledo

The famous "damascene" work, gold thread on oxidized black steel, is shown here from a shop. Here we watched an artisan painstakingly apply his craft.

Katie, a Narrow Street of Medieval Toledo

This image shows much of the reality of medieval Toledo; this is the way it was and still is!

Talavera Pottery, Katie, Toledo

The Talavera Pottery in Toledo comes from the nearby city of Talavera de la Reina. The ceramics go as far back as the times of Felipe II who used them in the Escorial. And the famous "Talavera" pottery in Mexico takes its name from this place. One could buy a complete set and then pay the very hefty price of shipping it home to the United States. Professor Flys' house in Arizona seemed to be a museum of the same.

Toledo Steel and Armor, Mark and the Knight

One source notes that Toledo steel was known since 500 B.C. and that it came to the attention of Rome when they encountered Hannibal and his troops using swords of steel from that region. An adaption of the same became standard in the Roman troops, the Toledo short sword. And the Spanish "conquistadores" were famed for their swords made in Toledo, the same said to not be good unless they could bend in half and deal a blow to steel helmets. The shops in Toledo abound with examples.

Toledo Steel and Armor, Katie and Her Knight in Shining Armor

So after this time in Toledo one breathes a sigh of exhaustion and relief and says "What an experience!"

MADRID ANEW

Saturday, July 18th Life in Madrid

Study, notes and reading. In the p.m. we went to the Prado once again and we saw what we missed before: the 19th century building, the Annex, not impressive on the outside, but inside, yes, to see the impressive "Guernica." After that we moved on later for a drink by the Neptune fountain near the Prado.

That night: the group was up until midnight with drinks, dinner and socializing at Jacinto's.

Sunday, July 19th.

Reading the "Quixote;" we are almost finished. We attended mass at the Colegio Mayor—I understood more because Padre Carlos was gone and a substitute spoke more clearly—we heard the Parable of the Mustard Seed.

There was a good Sunday lunch with garlic-roasted chicken, salad with garlic, onions, good tomatoes and olives. We ate with John, Sharon, Mike, Keah, Katie and Malana.

That p.m. we went to the Madrid zoo with Keah and Katie, Malana and Josie. There were three metro changes out to the south where it goes above ground, then a bus to the zoo. There was lots of green lawn and trees, but the water in the pools was stagnant. Elephants came close to us and we saw a pair of Pandas, baby tiger cubs, a fun parrot-macaw show, seals being fed with much splashing, etc. There were no problems on the long ride home and then to Jacinto's for "lomo de cerdo, salada y fritas, cerveza y vino."

Monday, July 20th.

Katie has a serious cough; we went to a local "clinic" in the Spanish Social Security Hospital, so we had to do paperwork and wait in pediatrics. Katie was scared by it all not understanding a word of what was being said. They took blood and she was in line for X-rays with emergency patients; then we went to the "caja" to pay. Her lungs and blood were okay; they gave her "jarabe," a cough medicine. It was in retrospect an interesting experience with Spanish socialized medicine. I thought it turned out well.

July 21ˢᵗ, 1987

A.M. Joe and I are almost finished with "The Quixote," then lunch at Jacinto's, a nap and drinks at the Colegio Mayor with Felisa, Miguel, John, Sharon and Mike.

Then Mark had a "date" with Keah, a quiet dinner at the "Gran Muralla"—fried chicken, delicious rice, "langostinos," and "vino." It was relaxing and fun. Later on everyone took the Metro to the "Plaza Colón" where we saw "La Pepa" and a flamenco show. It featured "flamenco sevillano" - two guitarists, one bongo, and "flamenco rumba." There were three girls dancing at once and "La Pepa," the diva star.

July 22, 1987

We did the last class of "Don Quiote." It was a really good experience with Joe. Although it was done in English translation with an abridged edition, it preserved some of my idealism about Spain! He will do a final paper-take home exam. I note that later on, thanks to the good will of Professor Angel Sánchez at Arizona State University, I taught the "Quixote" in Spanish to an upper division class in Tempe, the only time I would do this at ASU. Every professor of Spanish must have the experience!

That same day Professor Eugenio Suárez Galbán brought me an offer to do an introduction to the Brazilian folk-popular poetry or the "literatura de cordel" and a bilingual anthology in Spanish and Portuguese for his publishing house in Madrid. It would come out in the short period of one year after we got back to Arizona and I began working on the manuscript. It sounded like a neat, different project. I was thrilled and flattered at the possibility and would complete it during a sabbatical of 1989.

THE PRADO—PART II

In the p.m. we would have lunch at Jacinto's, a nap and a return visit to the Prado to see Goya's paintings as well as Picasso's "Guernica." Here are my notes from the experience and recollections of comments on it all by Michael Flys. Once again, photography was not permitted and the commercial slides I purchased are copyrighted, but the reader today can easily see it all by Googling the name of the painter or "el Prado."

GOYA

Goya did not do line sketches, but rather broad design for many paintings; the "cómicos" were to become "tápices" or tapestries, many used to decorate the most famous palaces in Spain. He was the lover of the Duchess of Alba.

He showed Queen María in the "family" portrait as "fea" but with "nice arms." She was the lover of Minister Godoy, "el favorito" in the famous family portrait; her son is between her and King Carlos and the son looks like Godoy.

Goya was not religious and was really opposed to the Church, so it enters little into his painting. But he had to paint the "Crucifición" to get into the Royal Academy of Painting; he was conforming. He married the daughter of the court painter to get his job at the court.

[An aside: here is Professor Michael Flys' joke about the Protestants in Spain who knock on the door of a Spaniard trying to convert him: "Mister, if I have the true religion in which I do NOT believe, how can I be expected to believe yours which is false?"]

Goya's "La Maja Desnuda"

It possibly depicts the Duchess of Alba. She deserted Goya so he painted "La Desnuda" from memory from "La Vestida."

Goya's "Costumbrista" scenes were done for the "cómicos" or "cartoons" which in turn became the tapestries which are found in public buildings and palaces all over Spain.

Goya's "La Familia Real"

The wife of the son was unmarried, so his "wife's" face is averted; there are exquisite details of fabrics, all in the French style he did not appreciate. He did not glamorize his royal subjects.

Queen Maria required copies of all the paintings to give to Godoy. Goya imitates Velásquez in putting his own portrait in the family portrait.

Goya's "May 2nd and 3rd, 1808"

The French soldiers depicted were Moroccan mercenaries. The painting expresses the sheer protest and terror of the war, its violence and deaths. The executioners are not in French uniform, but possibly in Russian. Goya was an "afrancesado" so he was not totally against the French. The Spanish nobility and aristocracy abandoned Spain, so the uprising and revolt were popular in nature, from the "pueblo."

Note: Many Spanish paintings were taken by the Duke of Wellington to England and the French destroyed many as well.

Goya's "Black" Period

Goya was very "depressed" and decorated his home or "quinta" with these paintings; they were not meant for public consumption. Now deaf and alone, he depicted his view of a corrupt Spain and its society. He slaps the paint on; there are no lines at all.

Picasso: "Guernica," 1936

The huge painting represents the first instance of a bombing of a civilian population. The painting is a protest of this inhumanity when the German "Luftwaft" bombed a major Spanish town. The painting was done and displayed in France. It later was taken to the U.S. and the New York Metropolitan Museum of Art "until Spain has democracy." At Franco's death it was returned to Spain. There is still opposition to the painting from those who supported Franco.

Parts of the painting depict: a dying horse, a woman screaming, a woman running to flee, a woman with a baby in her arms, a flower coming out of a sword, a bull, a window and a person viewing from outside.

TRIP TO SEGOVIA

Day Trip to Segovia, July 10th

Segovia and History

It was an important military town during Roman days and later came under the domain of the Moors and was a town famous for its wool.

There was a dispute in 1473. Isabel la Católica, now married to Fernando de Aragón, the half-sister of Henry IV of England, declared herself to be Queen of Castile and opposed Juana la Beltrana de la Cueva, the possible illegitimate daughter of Henry's wife the queen. So it was the "grandees of Spain" who named Isabella Queen. La Beltraneja was helped by her husband King Afonso V of Portugal, but she renounced in 1479. The marriage of Isabella and Fernando and the declaration by the "grandees" united Spain for the first time under the Catholic Kings. Isabella lived in Segovia at that time in the palace that was part of the Alcázar.

Segovia, the "Alcázar" Castle-Palace

The group retraced the bus route through the Guadarrama Mountains and then took a tunnel down the hill to Segovia. From the outskirts we saw the brown skyline of the old city with its Castillo and Alcázar. One could see the famous viaduct as well is at its other end. It is said that the city is in the form of a ship perched upon a large precipice 3000 feet high. The castle is at the confluence of two rivers.

View of the Old City and the Cathedral, Segovia

Equally impressive was the view of the Cathedral from the distance.

The Roman Aqueduct, Segovia

We saw the famous Roman aqueduct, 2392 feet long, 28 feet high, from the late 1st and early 2nd centuries A.D. It was done by Trajan the Roman Emperor.

The "Alcázar" Castle and Palace

Lateral view of the "Alcázar"

The "Alcázar" Castle and Palace was originally from the 13th century; it was renovated by Isabella's family the Trastamaras in the 15th century. It was beautifully kept and restored. Isabella set out from here in 1474 to be crowned Queen of Castile. In the 18th century it was made into an artillery academy. In 1862 it was gutted by fire.

A Miscellaneous note: King Felipe II, Hapsburg and son of Carlos V, was married for the 4th time here - to Ana of Austria.

The Tower of the "Alcázar"

Stained Glass Shield of Castile-León, the "Alcázar"

The Nobility and the Fight for Sovereignty in Toledo

The Plaza of Juan Bravo, Segovia

Years after Isabella La Católica's death and the arrival of Carlos V to Spain as King of Spain and the Holy Roman Empire (with its connection to Flanders) Spain experienced the "Comunero" Revolt which involved Spanish grandees who opposed Carlos V's Flemish friends and their weak efforts to control him. The communities of Toledo under Juan de Padilla and Segovia under Juan Bravo revolted but were defeated in 1521 and were executed. The "Old Quarter" of Segovia had unique exterior walls of Moorish design and the "Calle de Juan Bravo." The palaces in such plazas of Segovia belonged to the "grandees" and were decorated with coats of arms, There was Moorish design on the exterior; they reminded of the Alhambra and Sevila "mudéjar" styles.

"La Casa de los Picos," Segovia

A curious example of the architecture of the times was "Casa de los Picos." It made me think if "Romeo and Juliet" times in Italy.

243

The Romanesque Church of the Vera Cruz

The Romanesque Church of the "Vera Cruz," Segovia

After the palaces of the center of the old city we went to the "Iglesia de la Vera Cruz." It dates from 1208 and is highly unusual—it is polygonal, a fortress-church of the Knights of Templar or the Knights of the Holy Sepulcher. The interior room was used for a "vigil before knighthood," (one might think of Cervantes' parody of Don Quixote guarding his arms in a vigil at the fountain outside the inn) and there was a tower on the top. It seemed similar to "La Iglesia de San Marcos" in León. The style was Romanesque.

The "Retablo" de "La Iglesia de la Vera Cruz"

Church of the Tomb of San Juan de la Cruz and "Iglesia de la Vera Cruz," Segovia

While others were busy Keah and I discovered and then made a quick stop across the street to see the church and tomb of San Juan de la Cruz in the "Monasterio de los Carmelitas Descalzos."

The Tomb of San Juan de la Cruz

San Juan de la Cruz already mentioned in this text was of course a monk of the "Carmelitas Descalzos" the male order corresponding to the order established for females by Santa Teresa de Jesus in the environs of Ávila. San Juan enters the story not only for his untiring work in establishing the monasteries but for his place in Spanish Literature. "The Dark Night of the Soul" or "Noche Oscura del Alma" is not only recognized as a major religious work relating his mystical experiences, that is, the temporary but real union of the person with God, but since the work is in verse with prose commentary, it enters into Golden Age Poetry.

Painting of Santa Teresa de Jesus and San Juan de la Cruz, Segovia

The Picnic and the river, Outside Segovia

The Pouring of the Wine, the Picnic

Then the group, depending on the person, merrily or sleepily enjoyed the bus ride back to Madrid.

Mark J. Curran

"GIRA" AND PILGRIMAGE TO THE "SANCTUARIES"

July 23-26. Mark and Keah's Private "Gira"—the Pilgrimage and Trip North to Lourdes

It started on the bus out of Madrid, past the Plaza Mayor, la Puerta del Sol, Calle de Alcalá, and Avenida Castellanas. There was a slowdown in the traffic out of Madrid because of a protest by taxi drivers of the death of a driver.

We went east past Alcalá de Henares, Keah, Katie and me in the very back seat with a rough ride, but we made it fun. This is the town associated with Spain's most famous writer, Miguel de Cervantes Saavedra. He was born in Alcalá de Henares but spent most of his life in Madrid, Toledo, Valladolid, and Sevilla. 1547-1616. One should recall his adventures in the Battle of Lepanto versus the Turks, his capture and imprisonment in Árgel, his ransom and release, and finally the struggles to write and print his masterpiece "Don Quixote de la Mancha." This author's involvement with perhaps the most famous of Spain's writers is long and a bit curious. Having been introduced to the "Quixote" in an undergraduate survey of Spanish Literature at Jesuit Rockhurst College in Kansas City, Missouri, a more thorough "indoctrination" came at an unusual place—not Spain but the National University of Mexico. In the summer of 1962 I was enrolled in a seminar on "Cervantes—the Other Works." A Mexican professor with the comportment of an English Don from Oxford (he had in fact studied at Oxford) took us through Cervantes' life and exemplary novels and plays and such in English the Queen would have admired. It was only in graduate school where I experienced an incredibly fine course on the "Quixote," this time by a Jesuit priest talented in drama as well. The rest would be "history," teaching excerpts from the great novel in survey courses at A.S.U. and finally the entire work on one occasion. So these thoughts went through my mind as we passed Alcalá de Henares.

Trip to the "Sanctuaries," Olive Orchards in Spain

There were wheat fields as we left Madrid proper and as we passed through Castilla - la Mancha, Guadalajara, Castilla-León and on to Zaragoza. The land becomes extremely dry, even barren except along the rivers. Then we saw massive fields of olive orchards in Aragon.

We passed and saw from the bus the town of Calatayud, brown with its castle, minaret, and with a memorable church. The name is from "Kalat Ayub" from the name of a Moorish King; the town was built up against a greyish hillside; everything had the same color. This was the birthplace of Martial, 40-104 A.D., author of satires of the high society of Rome. The Church was Santa María la Mayor from the 16th century with "Mudéjar" influence and a minaret. Note: Calatayud appears in an episode in Spain's national epic, "El Poema de Mío Cid."

ZARAGOZA

Zaragoza is located in a plain with three rivers. The construction all seemed to be brown with a preponderance of brick buildings.

According to legend, in 40 A.D. the Virgin Mary appeared to the apostle Santiago who was discouraged at that time during his mission to Christianize Spain. He left the "pilar" or pillar on which the church is built. The "Virgen del Pilar" festival is the 12th of October.

In the 3rd century there is persecution of the Christians by Diocletian the Roman Emperor.

Then "Zaragossa" was ruled by the Moors, the Taifa Kings; they left the "Aljafería" part of the city.

Then it became the capital of the Kings of Aragón, famous for its "fueros" or rights of nobility.

It was under siege in 1808 by Napoleon's troops. The Spanish General Palafox led the defense; 50,000 were killed.

Our trip and tourism

The "Basílica de la Virgen del Pilar," Zaragoza

During our visit, the "Sé" or Cathedral was closed, "en obras." But we did see the "Basilica de Nuestra Señora del Pilar," 1677; some of its cupolas were painted by Goya and it contains a minute Gothic Statue of the "Virgen." She is the most important "santa" of all Spain.

The hotel in Zaragoza was adequate, a 3 - star, but the food was great for both meals: "fríos, paella, ternera con fritas, sandía, y vino claret" for the first and "sopa, huevo con mayonesa, ternera con salsa" for the second. The "ternera" tasted like good roast beef; then we enjoyed ice cream.

In addition to seeing the "Basilica del Pilar," we saw the Roman Wall dating from 24-27 B.C. done by Caesar Augustus. There was a great local market and then we walked the town, did some shopping and went home to the hotel. While at the Corte Inglés there was a downpour.

We met Lucho and María Zelaga from David Chiriquí, Panamá, he an engineer in Panamá. They of course reminded us of Mimi Lawyer, wife of good friend, colleague and professor of Spanish Jerry Lawyer at Ariona State. Mimi was from the same town and reminisced many times over its beauty. We would by the way have a very pleasant encounter with Mimi's sister and her husband in Madrid later in the trip. Lucho and María had visited the Durango area in Colorado and would become companions on the trip. Good fun.

Out of Zaragoza to Huésca

The Castle on the Hill, Huésca Province

Shortly, out of Zaragoza, we began the climb into the foothills of the Pyrenees and passed the province of Huésca. It seemed poor and dry, the poorest agricultural land we had seen thus far in Spain. Huésca is the capital of upper Aragón. It was established by a Roman officer around 77 B.C., was taken by the Moors in the 8th century but freed from the Moors by King Pedro I in 1096. It unfortunately has always been a "second" to Zaragoza. Huésca was besieged by the Republican Side for almost two years from 1936 to 1938 and was partially destroyed, as if the massive destruction by Napoleon's forces in the 19th century were not enough! From the highway we saw the ruins of BARLUENGA. This was the Monte Aragón Monastery dating from the 13th century; it was originally a fortress built by Sancho I to aid in the ousting of the Moors from Huésca. And it was not far from Barbastro, a town located at the foot of the Pyrenees foothills, with long, rugged valleys to the north. It was an important market center at the time of the Moorish invasion. The marriage of Ramón Berenguer IV and the Princess Petronila took place here in 1137 and this marked the union of Cataluña and Aragón.

BARBASTRO AND OPUS DEI

The Lake at Barbastro

Barbastro also is the birthplace of Padre Berenguer, founder of Opus Dei and Torre Ciudad, its shrine. We passed a large reservoir and dam and Torre Ciudad could be seen in the distance, an impressive sight high on a promontory by the lake.

The Church of Opus Dei, Barbastro

The place commemorates the "Vírgen de los Ángeles" from the 11th century and is the project of Berenguer, founder of Opus Dei. Inside the huge shrine we saw a video about Opus Dei, the Virgin's chapel, the confessionals and then just had a few minutes for a quick run down to the "Hermita" on the edge of a precipice overlooking the lake. Once again the student of Spanish Romanticism could do no less than think of Don Álvaro of "Don Álvaro o la Fuerza del Sino" when the tragic hero pitches himself over a cliff, saying "Infierno, trágame!" ["Hell, swallow me.!"] or something to that effect. I last read the play some years ago.

At some point there was a great "almuerzo" of "pan, vino, y paella," roasted chicken and potatoes and good caramel ice cream, and social time with Lucho and María.

ACROSS THE PYRENEES

Small Town in the Pyrenees

We were winding through foothills of the Pyrennes with brown, stone villages with churches or a "casa solar" in the main plaza.

Peaks of the Pyrenees

Then there was a gradual change to view the steep peaks of the Pyrenees, rushing streams below the road and a cloudburst before the "Túnel de Bisela." There was water streaming all around us, falls rushing out on both sides of the road, and it was a bit scary. At one point the scene did seem to match the San Juans of Colorado. We passed through quaint mountain villages with small hotels and some soaked campers.

The Border and Entrance into France

At this point we entered France at Bisela and Androguet after the long tunnel. It was in total fog and one could scarcely see the road. We stopped at a small café at the entrance into France where none spoke Spanish, or perhaps refused to speak this language. It was a new experience with road signs in French, a new language and new currency. I asked for a "pression," a draft beer.

Subsequently there was a gorgeous drive to Lourdes, the road with high ridges to the side and lush and green meadows abounded. I said "I have never seen such greenness anywhere!" The small towns alongside the road were pretty as well. There were milk cows, hay and green pastures.

FRANCE AND LOURDES

Katie, Keah, the Basilica of Lourdes

We were amazed at the size of the place with its many stores, the nice hotel the Miramonte but with subpar food at least for the introductory meal that night (the French sauces were a disappointment). We left the meal early to join the procession and heard many languages during the recitation of the Rosary. All process with banners during the procession, and each decade of the Rosary is introduced in a different language. We were exhausted after the travel, the procession and all, and to bed.

The Cross and Basilica, Lourdes

The next morning there was breakfast of "café au lait" and what else? French Croissants! We went immediately to the Basilica where along with the other pilgrims we saw the slide show about Bernadette and the apparitions. We remained in the same Basilica for mass with English Catholics.

The Grotto of the Apparitions

Mass was followed by a visit to the Grotto for adoration, to the spring for the "holy" water, and to the Via Crucis for photos. Katie actually did two or three steps on her knees! (I should remind her of this today).Then it was time for lunch, once again to the French restaurant, this time with good soup, salad, roast chicken or "coq au vin," and ice cream. This was followed by a sudden rush by our bus driver and guide to leave Lourdes. All of a sudden we were on a four lane zooming along parallel to the Pyrenees with magnificent farming land—mainly incredible corn all tasseled out—all a deep green. It seemed very prosperous all the way to Bayonne.

SAN SEBASTIÁN AND THE BASQUE COUNTRY

We would now enter that famous region of Spain simply called the "Basque Country." It is replete with famous places: the Cantabrian coast, the Caves of Altamira, Bilbao (birthplace of Miguel de Unamuno), Covadonga, Guernica, Irún, Oviedo, and Aspeitia or Loyola, the home and fiefdom of the family of the future founder of the Jesuits San Ignacio de Loyola. And then we would travel down into Old Castile ("Castilla la Vieja") and Burgos, Vitoria and then "home" to Madrid.

The Bay at San Sebastián, Basque Country

We crossed the border from France into San Sebastián; it seemed huge and industrial, but was interesting at the port which was busy with shipping and at the "Plaza de la Concha," its main plaza. The city features the Bahía de la Concha, is a tourist capital and also a center of Basque separatism. One recalls the ETA and problems.

Don Quixote and Sancho in Basque Country

The Basque Region of Northern Spain we would now enter brings to mind the Spanish writer of note and one of the country's main intellectuals, Miguel de Unamuno, 1864-1936. He was born in Bilbao, took his Ph.D. at the University of Madrid, and was Rector of the University of Salamanca in later life. Unamuno to me, as per an entire one semester seminar at Saint Louis University dedicated solely to a reading of his "life and works," was a difficult pill to swallow. Perhaps it was his personality, but I can only give my own opinion, shared by many but disputed by just as many. One cannot deny his intellectual weight in the twentieth century in Spain, but he carried a lot of baggage. First of all, pardon me, he was Basque with a traditional independent and stubborn Basque demeanor and he was proud of it and let everyone know it. And his arrogance knew no bounds. He was a thorn in the side to anyone who disputed his opinions. His most important work was "El Sentimiento Trágico de la Vida" or "The Tragic Sense of Life," a book claimed by many to be "philosophy" but by others to be simply "a way of thinking." A professor I respected most at Saint Louis University, Dr. Edward Sarmiento, took the latter view: Unamuno was a "great thinker." I think it is all a matter of semantics: Unamuno was unlike Ortega y Gasset (a contemporary) who actually developed a philosophical system and explained it in his book "Historia como Sistema;" Unamuno rather wrote what I would call a complicated and enormous treatise with one basic idea: reason tells us there can be no God; our heart and "being" make us

261

WANT God to exist. And this is the "tragic sense of life," that is, we want God to exist but all our rational process tells us no. I realize this is a great simplification, but I think it hits the mark. But what makes Unamuno unique was that I believe this crisis, both intellectual and emotional, became a true "idée fixe" and the main theme of many novels including his famous "San Manuel Bueno, Mártir." We read several of the novels and they all seemed to be a "variation on a theme." I would have shaken in my boots to be face to face with this person, as most in Spain indeed felt in university exams before his Professor's chair at the University of Salamanca where he was "Catedrático" or Full Professor of Greek.

Politically it was simpler; Unamuno was a liberal, a staunch Republican in Republican Spain, and then a victim of Franco. After exile in France like many other famous Spanish intellectuals including Picasso and a return to Spain, he died at the beginning of the tragic Spanish Civil War. But he exemplifies the Basque Intellectual in Spain. A much more pleasant person is to come.

Tomorrow to Aspeitia- Loyola in the Basque Country

I wrote in the midst of all this: "Next time we must get to Navarra, Pamplona, and Roncevalles—the pass where the Basques slaughtered Charlemagne's rear guard of knights—a different version of the "Chanson de Roland" and its counterpart in Brazil—the Brazilian folk-popular poem "A Morte dos Doze Pares da França." I think the Basque version is the historically accurate."

Some Aspects of the Basque Country:

The Basque Country or as it is known in Spanish as "Vascongadas" or "País Vasco" is really three provinces in northern Spain: Viscaya, Guipúzcoa and Álava.

The Basque mountains, some 1500 meters or 5000 feet, face the true Pyrenees and not the Cantabrian range which is west and includes the group of mountains called Picos de Europa which reach some 8000 feet and where the skiing goes on.

The language is "Euskara" or Basque. Some unique and perhaps colorful aspects of their culture:

The trunk cutting game "aizkolari"

The rock lifters: "panlankari"

Pole throwing

Pelota—this is "jai alai."

One of the famous places is Covadonga in the middle of the Picos de Europa. This was where Pelayo revolted against the Moors in 718 AD and defeated the Muslims in 1722. He was elected King of Asturias with its singular claim to fame—it was never conquered by the Moors!

Also in Basque Country is Guernica; Picasso's painting immortalizes the first bombing of a civilian population in any war. It was bombed by the Luftwaft in 1937.

ASPEITIA—LOYOLA AND THE "TORRE-CASA" OF SAN IGNACIO LOYOLA

The Countryside on the way to Aspeitia-Loyola

The scenery down to Loyola from San Sebastián was truly gorgeous—all green velvet hills, hay stacked in the fields, cattle and sheep in the meadows. Then after we turned off toward Aspeitia, there were taller, steeper hills, still all green, a stream in between, sheep high in the meadows, but now we were in pine forest also dense with "robles" and "hayas" or oak and maple.

Aspeitia is now known as Loyola. The town has the "casa solar" of the Loyola family. Ignacio's dates are from 1491-1556. A few impressionistic facts as to the man: he was a young, feisty, "caballero" of his aristocratic class and received the call to arms in local battles. Then he was wounded at Pamplona, suffering damage to his leg after being hit by a spent cannon ball. During the long convalescence while reading the "Lives of the Saints" he experienced a religious vision and conversion and subsequently traveled to Monserrate on a pilgrimage in 1522. He was then living in the cave at Manresa (Cataluña) where he began to write the "Ejercicios Espirituales" or "Spiritual Excercises." Then he did a pilgrimage to Jerusalem in 1523, traveled to Paris in 1525 and London in 1530. He had joined his "compañeros" Diego Laínez and Francisco Javier and all were ordained in 1537. All did a pilgrimage to Rome swearing loyalty to the Pope and the Society of Jesus was formed in 1540. He was canonized in 1622, the same time as Francisco Xavier and Santa Teresa de Jesús.

We did a quick tour of Loyola, the old castle, the modern basilica and attended mass there. Some high points are depicted in the following photos. The perhaps surprisingly large amount of space they take in this book can be attributed in part to the fact that this author was trained in Jesuit schools for seven years, and perhaps a little bit of their instruction stuck with me. I know that I would have taken Jesuit Philosophy and Theology a lot more seriously on the undergraduate level had I already seen his home and castle in Spain.

Front of the Basilica of San Ignacio de Loyola

Side of the Basilica and the Green Hills of Loyola

Candelabra and Main Altar, Interior of the Basilica

Close up, Main Altar of the Interior of the Basilica

Casa-Torre of the Loyola family, Castilian, Basque, French and English

Bronze of the Fallen Soldier Ignacio de Loyola

Loyola at Prayer

The "Virgen de Monserrate" Loyola's Inspiration

VITORIA

Vitoria is the capital of Álava Province with beautiful mountain scenery, still an emerald green. There were several industrial towns with major factories. We came down a steep, hair-pinned road into rolling foothills, then into the grain region of Vitoria. There were still many road signs in Basque.

Vitoria is a cereal covered plateau; it looked like Salamanca's plains. It was founded in 1181 by Sancho the Wise, King of Navarra. We saw the façade of the Gothic 14th century cathedral. Then we traveled down into Castilla la Vieja to the historic and beautiful city called Burgos.

BURGOS

The City Wall—Entrance to Burgos

We were now in the old provinces of Castile and León and arrived at one of their most famous and historic places: Burgos! The only problem was it was an incredibly short twenty minute stop! The entrance to the city has the Coat of Arms of Castile. All is in a river valley near 3000 feet in altitude; this is the Río Arlanzón of Spain's Epic "Poema del Cid." An aside: an old friend from Saint Louis University, Mario Santizo raised in Guatemala, high school with the Jesuits in

Belize and undergraduate and graduate work at SLU, for years ran the University of Iowa Spanish Summer School in Burgos.

Burgos: Its Literary History

This is the geographic region for the beginning of the Spanish Epic Poem, "El Poema de Mío Cid" and its hero Rodrigo Díaz de Vivar, a village only nine kilometers from Burgos. The poem is present in all the anthologies of Spanish Literature and is a "must" read even on the undergraduate level. It tells the ups and downs of Spain's great national hero who was instrumental in early battles by the Christians to defeat the Moors and regain the country for Spain. But it is much more because it details the relationship between vassal and lord, soldier and king, knight in shining armor and wife. Even though a successor to the epic tradition of Homer and Virgil, it departs from the classic rhetoric and verse of the former and is written in the vernacular Spanish of medieval Spain. The tombs of El Cid and his wife Doña Ximena are in the Cathedral of Burgos.

The old region of Castile-León is also the region of a certain part of the old "Romances" of medieval and early modern Spain. Although the themes of the "romances" included famous poems from Andalucía like "Abenámar, Abenarmar," many of its most famous tell of the times of the Cid and the Reconquest in the north. Perhaps the most famous is "La Jura en Santa Gadea" when the Cid challenges his lord and king Alfonso to swear on the Holy Bible that he did not kill his own brother Sancho in order to gain power. A popular and cinematic aside: most westerners know of this business through the Hollywood version of "El Cid" with Charton Heston and Sophia Loren. Although glitzy and based much more on the legends surrounding the Cid rather than history, the film did indeed capture much of the spirit and tensions of the times.

Later Literature of the Region and the Times: "Castilla la Vieja" or Old Castile:

One sees the poetry of the cleric Gonzalo de Berceo 1195-1265 of La Rioja-Castilla la Vieja-Aragón. "Milagos de Nuestra Señora."

Jorge Manrique 1440-1479. His father was, like the Cid in earlier times, the "Condestable de Castilla." He was "Maestre de la Orden de Santiago" and fought against Moors in Granada. Jorge's poem is one of the great works of Spanish poetry of late medieval-early Renaissaince times, an elegiac tribute to his father: "Coplas por la Muerte de su Padre."

History of Burgos

Burgos was founded in 951 with the Roman name "Caput Castellae." Years later it was selected by Fernán González to become the capital of the then "Condado de Castilla." This would be the time and place of "El Cid." In 1037 Fernando I united Castilla, León and Aragón under one kingdom and then battled the Moors to win back Madrid in 1083 and Toledo in 1085. This is the early phase of the famous Spanish "Reconquista" which would only end in Granada in 1492.

1026-1099. Rodrigo Díaz de Vivar, El Cid, served Sancho II, then Alfonso VI; he was banished for his suspicions of the King and the King's jealousy. He married Ximena, cousin of the King. He served first as a mercenary for the Moorish King of Saragossa. He battled and defeated the Count of Barcelona and then captured Valencia in 1094, using Moorish troops. He was later defeated by the Moors at Cuenca and died in 1099. Ximena held Valencia until 1102 when she left and burned the city and took El Cid's body with her. Legend has been kind to him.

In 1492 Burgos lost its place as capital of Castilla to Valladolid but remained an important center.

In 1812 Burgos was a French stronghold under Napoleon which resisted siege by the Duke of Wellington and it was "blown up" by José Bonaparte in 1813.

Later, the "Movimiento Nacional" set up a provisional government here in 1936 against the Republicans, and it was here that Francisco Franco was declared "head of state."

The Cathedral of Burgos

The Cathedral of Burgos

It is the third largest in Spain after Sevilla and Toledo. It was begun in 1221 with French, German, and Spanish architects along with those from Flanders in Belgium. It combines flamboyant Gothic and Spanish "Mudéjar."

Scenes from the Cathedral or Burgos

The Sarcophagi of the "Condestables de Castilla," the Cathedral of Burgos

The "Capilla de los Condestables" was done in 1482 with Carrara marble tombs. It contains the tombs of El Cid and Doña Ximena. They are located on the floor in a central part of the church which is surrounded by a large steel "reja" or high screen.

Tomb of "El Cid Campeador," Cathedral of Burgos

While pondering the Latin and Old Spanish inscribed on the tomb and serenely thinking of classes in Spanish Literature we suddenly heard the engine of the bus and the honking of its horn. The gates of the "reja" were closed and locked behind us. Facing the fate of that cold stone floor in the Cathedral, we shouted and yelled for the sacristan who did come with jangling keys, freeing us to continue the journey. It was all a bit of a fright.

Travel after Burgos and "Home" to Madrid

The Bus "Home" to Madrid

There were rolling hills, dry and barren, and some wheat lands on down to Madrid. Sixty-one kilometers out of the city we hit the "caravana" or rush traffic heading out of Madrid anticipating the August vacation; traffic was at a stop. Routine was soon back to normal on the return.

LAST DAYS IN MADRID

July 28th.

Classic Guitars Made in Madrid

We took the Metro to the city center to the guitar shop. I played two instruments: a "Serie Primera" and a "Guitarra de Cámara." The first was a Ramírez Guitar made of "palo de santo;" the fret action was higher than at home and the guitar was no "prettier" to look at than my Di Giorgio Rosewood guitar from Brazil in 1966. But the tuning and tone were perfect even in the high ranges, a "true" tone.

I then played a $3,200 "Guitarra de Cámara" and thought I had arrived in guitar heaven. The volume and "brilliance" of tone were apparent. I have not played such a fine instrument since although in 2002 I purchased a fine Manuel Rodriguez guitar from his Madrid shop. I played sitting on a broken down chair downstairs in the warehouse. It was an incredible shop for music, Flamenco methods and books; I thought Flamenco Guitar was all learned "orally," not so at all.

A Madrid Moment: the Metro to the "Parque de Atracciones"

Mark and Katie, the Entrance to the Metro, Madrid

Keah, Katie, Tamara and I took the Metro and three changes to Bataan Station on the southwest side of the city. The park seems like a U.S. carnival and amusement park combined with the impression of a slightly run down Disneyland. The rides are fine, up to date and well maintained. In fact the park is quite fun. You pay an admittance fee of 115 pesetas and buy a "pulsera" or wristband which allows you to enter all parts of the park and ride for 45 pesetas a ride.

The kids, Katie and Tamara, did a cute merry go round with elephants, ostriches, etc.; then we did the "Mini 7 Picos," a kids' roller coaster. That was enough for me. Then to the "Twister"—it whirls you around and up and down. Then there was a funny "jungle boat" ride through brackish water, with hippos and elephants, all coming apart, black natives needing paint, all very splotchy. It was sort of like Disney's Jungle Cruise; Keah and Katie loved it.

Then we went to a riverboat where you have to walk on rollers, on a turning barrel, on boards sliding in opposite directions, and on a spongy surface. It was crowded and super-hot.

Next was the very high Ferris wheel; its only connection to my fear of heights was that you could see the Plaza de España from the top. We all had sweaty hands.

Then we went to a funny "scare house," a real flop. Our car broke down inside.

We all had lots of "granizado" or lemon slush and popcorn or "palomitas."

Then there was a House of Mirrors, real fun and cute; they distort you in 12 different ways. The House also includes a "laberinto" with mirrors, tricky to traverse.

Then we went to the "race cars" where you drive electric, battery powered roadsters at a good clip; it was fun, we scooted right along.

Keah and I did most of the rides with Katie and Tamara. It was one of Katie's favorite times on the trip and she absolutely glowed with happiness. It was good to see her so happy. It turned out to be a good thing that we took the initiative and invited Tamara.

July 29th.

Grading, talk to Suárez Galbán about the book and shopping at the Corte Inglés.

Chinese food with Katie, Keah and Josie. Nap in p.m.

July 30.

Shopping on the "Gran Vía" in the p.m. It included taking photos of downtown Madrid together with Michael, Felisa and Tamara. There was shopping at Prado Shops and "Lladró" on Gran Vía where we made our most important purchases in Spain: a beautiful Lladró statue of El Greco and a Flamenco Dancer for Katie. That evening there was dinner at Jacinto's and socializing in the lounge and some quiet time for me and Keah.

DAY TRIP TO EL ESCORIAL

August 1st

Main Entrance, El Escorial

It was designed in 1559 as both a monastery and a royal palace marking Spain's place in the Christian world. It came during the period of the Counter-Reformation and Felipe II's role as a "defender of the faith" against the Protestant Reformation. So the huge edifice was first a Hieronymite monastery but is now run by the Augustinians. Today it is monastery and museum. Felipe II also had in mind it being the necrotarium or tomb of the Spanish kings and that has been largely the case since the 16th century, the first king of renown being Felipe's own father the great Carlos V of Spain and the Holy Roman Empire in much of the first half of the 16th century, the time when Spain came to control much of the old and new worlds. The design of the entire complex—a portico and interior patio followed by another portico and patio before the actual building itself is said to have similarities to the Alhambra in Granada, the Alcázar in Sevilla and perhaps the original Temple of Solomon in ancient Judea! Felipe gave instructions to guarantee the place would be noted for its simplicity of line (the quadrangle with interior patios) and severity of tone.

Mark's Photo, Painting of a Medieval Battle, El Escorial

Mark's Photo, One of Goya's "Tápices" or Tapestries, El Escorial

It is a huge art gallery as well with most of the European masters represented and an incredibly beautiful library. The rooms of the old palace and residence are impressive as well. We took our time and saw almost all of it.

The entire summer school group took the Herranzo bus to the town of El Escorial and then did a tour of this famous, outstanding monument to Felipe II the Hapsburg. There was a nice lunch in an outdoor café—"paella y ternera."

DAY TRIP TO "EL VALLE DE LOS CAÍDOS"

The Base of the Cross and the Plaza, Valle de los Caídos

We boarded the bus from El Escorial and headed to Francisco Franco's funerary monument the Valle de los Caídos, did a walk around the rather formidable but gloomy place which we found cold, austere and not recalling a pleasant time in Spain.

Basically this is an underground church topped with a thirty ton plain concrete cross. Inside is the long nave of the church with Franco's tomb at the head. Supposedly a monument for the fallen in Spain's tragic civil war of 1936 to 1939 it is interesting that the only two soldiers enterred are Franco himself and Primo de Rivera the founder of the Falange Party. Some have called it Fascist design and architecture and not a bit beautiful. It is noted that Republican prisoners of war were used as labor to carve the huge underground edifice from the quarry.

The Cross and Entrance to the Mausoleum, Valle de los Caidos

After this ever so brief visit, we happily boarded the bus and arrived "home" to the Colegio Mayor and pleasant talk with an Argentine from Buenos Aires, a chat with Marta, Jacinto and Encarnación and Padre Carlos.

Miscellaneous Notes of the Final Days in Madrid

El Palacio Real

This place is historically important in Madrid and we spent several hours touring it. Once again, photos were not allowed and the commercial slides are copyrighted, so Google "Palacio Real" to see it all. This huge edifice with large patios and impressive gardens rests on the east side of Madrid's Manzanares River. As with much of Spain its origin is ancient and complicated: it was originally a Moorish fort on the site linked to the Moorish leader of Córdoba and then Toledo. After the conquest ended in 1492 it was largely ignored by the Spanish until the 16th century when Carlos V built the beautiful Alcázar. Recall that the capital and court of Spain had just recently been moved to Madrid from Toledo. The building had a history of its own and was one of the major buildings of Spain and in some degree all Europe. The building burned in the 1700s and was rebuilt by Felipe V and became the main palace for the Bourbon dynasty which rules until today. It is no longer a royal residence but is used for state functions. The place is massive and I recall the grand entrance, the royal throne room, the pharmacy, the chapel, bedrooms of the royal family, but most importantly the Armor Museum considered one of the best of its kind in the world. There were not only many complete armored knights, but even armored horses and dogs! We spent the good part of a day seeing the place. Meant to rival Versailles in its elegance, and highly French in character, it seemed more just than a royal palace of Spain.

The "Corte Inglés"

This was the principal store visited by our student group as well as Madrileños. It certainly was equal to anything in a modern shopping center in the United States at the time. We had little need for its stuff and thus used it little, but it has everything you could want including massive crowds, especially during the five to eight p.m. hours. We did buy a few tourist gifts and tried for shoes and clothes for Katie. It was a major shopping place for the Spaniards; it does not close for the 3 hour pm. siesta. The chain is all over Spain and we visited other stores a time or two, including one during a heavy rain storm in Zaragoza. There is always a super market, a barber shop, a bookstore, etc. One could say it is the equivalent of a U.S. mall in one store. We learned a lot about others in our group, adults and kids. They were much more into shopping and material things.

Joe's Place

My tutorial student for the "Don Quixote" class was Joseph Allred. This was his place and "gift" to us. It was a Chinese Restaurant near the Corte Inglés at Argüellas Plaza. The name was appropriate for the theme—"The Great Wall" or "La Gran Muralla." It was quiet and with reasonable prices. We ate on different occasions tasty rice, almond chicken, Chinese fried chicken, shrimp tempura, and often accompanied with a good "Claret" wine. And we always sat by large aquariums. It was a welcome respite from the crowds and heat of Madrid in the Spanish p.m. The "menu" was 500 pesetas or about $4.00 U.S. In all honesty it agreed with us so much because of the quiet atmosphere and some of the best tasting food we experienced in Spain.

The Final Student Party

The Last Party with the Students, "El Colegio Mayor"

A Happy Group with Jacinto, "El Colegio Mayor"

Tamara and Katie dancing "Sevillanas"

Although I did not talk much about individual students on the trip, I certainly found them interesting. We had different ages and types, fun-seeking ASU coeds, three or four Hispanics and Latin Americans wanting to experience their cultural roots, and a few adults along for the experience. We certainly went our separate ways on the nights out because the kids were at the clubs, concerts and late night "tertulias" on the streets. We did socialize with them however in the many informal parties at the hostels or hotels on the "giras" and especially at Jacinto's Place in the Colegio Mayor dormitory. It was very nice to be just "faculty" and not "director" as I was in Guatemala in 1976 and 1977. Michael Flys had the experience and the know how to create a good blend of learning, tourism and fun.

The Last Day

Keah is still very sick from a lingering bout with the flu and respiratory problems, but a little better, well enough to go to the "Casa Gallega" for our last dinner with the group. It was quite a feast with "caldo gallego, pimientos de padrón, champiñon, pollo al ajillo, solomillo, guisantes y zanahorias, y helado." The wine was "Ribeiro" and then the Spanish tradition of "queimada" demonstrated by our leader Michael Flys. Thus ended the culinary, social and cultural adventure in Spain.

The Journey Home

Mark and Katie Heading Home on TWA

Final Thoughts on Spain—A Review of Part II of the Book

As we headed back home across the Atlantic on the TWA jet, I wrote these notes while it was all fresh in my mind. This book is only being written some twenty-seven years later! I wrote . . .

"The churches, palaces, monasteries and castles we saw were up to expectations. It was a positive experience in that we saw the roots from the past—the Roman, the Romanesque, Moorish, Gothic, Plateresque, Renassaince, Baroque, Neo-Classic and modern. It was a successful business.

"The ten week time in Portugal and Spain included a total of some five weeks of travel, and it all was a success. In Portugal there was Lisbon, Belém, Cascais, Alcobaça, Nazaré, Óbidos, Leiria, Coimbra (o Porto), Viana do Castelo, Guimarães, and the bus through southwest Portugal to Badajoz in Spain.

"In Spain there was the original bus trip through Extremadura, past Sevilla and on to Málaga. In Spain we saw Málaga, Torremolinos, Mijas, Palos, Granada, Córdoba, Sevilla, Mérida, Cáceres, Salamanca, Santiago de Compostela, Pontevedra, León, Simancas and Madrid. Day trips from Madrid were the important day trips to Ávila, Segovia, Toledo, el Escorial and Valle de los Caídos. The side trip for the Currans, a sort of religious pilgrimage, was the bus tour featuring Zaragoza, Huesca, Torreciudad, Pirineos, Lourdes, Bayonne, San Sebastián, Loyola, Vitoria, Burgos and back to Madrid.

"Recollection of Specific Places and Reactions:

"In Málaga the Corpus Christi feast day and the "Fiesta de la Malagueta" with the bull fight, the Sevillanas dancing and the Arabic horses were highlights. We enjoyed parties in the Flys' room in Málaga at the hostel; the gatherings were informal and included the adults and the college kids.

"In the "Gira" or travels to diverse cities that followed I loved the quiet time for socializing in the Hostels and especially at the "Colegio Mayor" later in Madrid. That WAS our social life in Spain. We enjoyed the older students, but Katie especially loved all those college coeds who fawned over her and Tamara.

"Torremolinos was a European and Spanish phenomenon—topless and with icy water. The sea was pretty.

293

"We loved the Alhambra and the Generalife but had to overlook the immense parking lot full of tour buses and the crowds. The immense beauty of the place overcomes the small irritations mentioned. Granada is impressive and dramatic with the above as well as its Cathedral of the Catholic Kings.

"There was immense satisfaction is seeing Córdoba's mosque and the Catholic cathedral inside and also the quaint "Judaría." It was a thrill to see this famous place.

"The scenery of the countryside in southern Spain was pleasant as well: the endless, rolling hills of wheat, gira-soles, olive tree groves, and some cork. The hills on the way to Granada were pretty as were the stark white towns in Andalucía on the hillsides. And the black bulls in the pastures.

There is nothing comparable to all we saw in Sevilla. Enough said.

The history and impressive monuments of Salamanca, Santiago de Compostela, León, Ávila and Toledo were a delight. The surprises of the "Santuaries" Trip were also welcome—Zaragoza, Loyola and Burgos.

"We appreciated the greenness of Galicia, the "hórreos," the "rías" at Pontevedra, and the "viñas." In my mind it did not quite match Portugal. But I would never have missed it!

Interaction with People in Spain

"We were always in a tourist situation so we met few Spaniards on a personal level. When we did it was a treat! There seemed to be a definite harshness, a survival of the fittest attitude in stores, bars, cafés, etc. where we found waiters to be indifferent or even rude at times, more so than in Portugal. If you needed help or wanted information it really seemed to pain them. Very different from Brazil! I think once again they knew we were "temporary" tourists and knew they would not see us again. I'm sure the "regulars" got better treatment.

"This comment is totally personal and perhaps impressionistic. The people did not ever seem to me to be as jovial as the Brazilians, although the Spanish were great lovers of the "tertulia" and socializing that would go far into the night and early morning hours. The music was pleasant with the flamenco and Málaga's "Sevillanas." The atmosphere simply seemed to be a bit more serious. I'm thinking this observation could well just be my own experience and not really the case. Other opinions and perspectives are needed.

Speaking Spanish.

"I communicated very well on the whole especially with Nico in Salamanca and Mimi Lawyer's husband Javier on the phone, but was horribly frustrated with Padre Carlos and Jacinto at the Colegio Mayor in Madrid. This no reflection on the latter; the gamut from crystal clear diction and pronunciation to its opposite is not just an aspect of Spain. In a related circumstance, I was extremely frustrated at the "Zarzuela" in Madrid because I understood so little. And a big disappointment in Spain was the rule that all movies are dubbed; thus all American movies were in Spanish rather than in Spanish subtitles. It really cut down on Keah, Katie and my own social life.

The Food.

"With my fragile constitution I was extremely careful and as a result had minimal digestive problems, but several of the local dishes, regional treats and all, do not yet appeal to me. Most "tapas" were not my cup of tea. I enjoyed the bread, the salads, the beef "filetes," some fish, flan and ice creams. And also lots of different wines. I really liked the "caldo gallego" and "sopa de pescado o mariscos," but could not manage the maneuvers to eat the small "cangrejos," I thoroughly enjoyed the "café con leche" and there was good socializing at breakfast time. And I mention elsewhere that the food and drink and socializing at Jacinto's Place in the dorm saved the day as well as the great Chinese food at the "Gran Muralla."

"The "Menú del Día"

We tried to adapt to the almost mid-afternnon "menu," but with its food and wine in such quantities, it made for sleepy customers. I'm sure as one stays longer in Spain this would become the custom and a great pleasure! Is this why the Spanish still maintained the long siesta hour in those years? A "plato combinado" seemed to be a good solution when we sometimes split the plate. You get soup or salad, fish, meat, dessert and "vino de la casa."

We ate breakfast at 8:30, a snack of one-half sandwich or donut at 11:30, the main meal at 2:30 or 3:30, drinks and "aceitunas" at 7:30-8:30, and supper at 9:00 or 9:30. But we never did the late "cena" at 11:00 or 12:00 and the disco routine to 4 or 5 a.m. We slept very well on our own system, but we really never did get into the Spanish schedule. Once again I'm sure this all would change with an extended stay in Spain. And part of the reason one travels is to experience the new, "verdad?"

Other Matters

"There was great, efficient transportation on the Metro and "circulares" in Madrid, but it was a bit scary at times. The lines and cars were old and the stations were hot in that Madrid August. Now we know why thousands stream out of Madrid during the August vacation month and the traffic jams getting out of town make it on the TV news!

"Newpapers. I enjoyed "El País" more than "ABC." The editorial page and really all the articles are much more literary, philosophical and even poetic than in the U.S.

I loved the Prado; it met and surpassed all my hopes. Twenty-five years of study and teaching of Spanish came to fruition.

"We liked the sidewalk cafés and bars on Avenida Castellanas near the Correos, the Prado and Plaza Colón, and the flamenco music. One could add the cafés in Salamanca, its Plaza Mayor with the "Tunas", and the cafés and bars in Compostela and León.

This is where I fell asleep on the airplane. I have debated whether to retain these few observations in the text. I think they will stay.

EPILOGUE

As mentioned in the beginning, this was the trip that "filled in the gaps" for me. Intensive study of Spanish and Brazilian Portuguese languages, teaching the same regularly over the years, teaching the Introduction to Spanish Literature and especially the Spanish Civilization and Luso-Brazilian Civilization courses were all good preparation. I arrived in Portugal and Spain knowing what to look for and excited to see it. In this sense the entire time was a great success. We indeed saw the highlights of Portugal and Spain and were overwhelmed by the immensity of what they offered in terms of landscape, art, palaces, castles and more. I tried then and have tried in this manuscript to "marry" the academic and the travel and whenever possible to relate what I knew best—major literary and artistic figures to their places in Portugal but mainly in Spain.

As for the interaction with the people, it was really what should have been expected—we were travelers, tourists and teachers within the confines of an American Summer Study Program in three months' time. Longer stays in Spain and Portugal under other circumstances would perhaps have resulted in truly living and interacting with the people.

What I do know is that the trip incredibly enriched my final fourteen years of teaching at ASU and thereby enriched the experience offered to the students. When I taught "El Poema del Cid," "Coplas por la Muerte de su Padre," the Golden Age plays of Lope de Vega or Calderón de la Barca, the poetry of Garcilaso de la Vega, Fray Luis de León, and Luis de Góngora, Miguel de Cervantes' "Don Quixote,", the 19th century literature of el Duque de Rivas, Gustavo Adolfo Bécquer, Zorilla and the romantics, and in the twentieth century Miguel de Unamuno and García Lorca, artist and place were united. And I of course showed all these places plus the paintings from the Prado from the hundreds of slides taken or purchased on the trip. And the history of it all came alive. Once again I say thank you to Michael Flys and wife Felisa for the opportunity.

And lastly, thank you Keah and thank you Katie for coming along, giving moral support and, yes, expanding your own horizons. When you were happy it added to my own joy.

ABOUT THE AUTHOR

Mark Curran is a retired professor from Arizona State University where he worked from 1968 to 2011. He taught Spanish and Brazilian Portuguese languages and their respective cultures. His research specialty was Brazil's folk-popular literature or as it is known in Brazil, the "literatura de cordel," and he has published many research articles and thirteen books on the subject in Brazil, the United States and Spain. Subsequent books are mainly autobiographical and/ or reflect civilization classes taught at ASU: the series "Stories I Told My Students."

Published Books

A Literatura de Cordel. Brasil. 1973.
Jorge Amado e a Literatura de Cordel. Brasil. 1981
A Presença de Rodolfo Coelho Cavalcante na Moderna Literatura de Cordel. Brasil. 1987
La Literatura de Cordel—Antología Bilingüe—Español y Portugués. España. 1990
Cuíca de Santo Amaro Poeta-Repórter da Bahia. Brasil. 1991.
História do Brasil em Cordel. Brasil. 1998
Cuíca de Santo Amaro—Controvérsia no Cordel. Brasil. 2000
Brazil's Folk-Popular Poetry—"a Literatura de Cordel"—a Bilingual Anthology in English and Portuguese. USA. 2010
The Farm—Growing Up in Abilene, Kansas, in the 1940s and the 1950s. USA. 2010
Retrato do Brasil em Cordel. Brasil. 2011
Coming of Age with the Jesuits. USA. 2012
Peripécias de um Pesquisador "Gringo" no Brasil nos Anos 1960, ou, À Cata de Cordel. USA. 2012
Adventures of a 'Gringo' Researcher in Brazil in the 1960s. USA, 2012
A Trip to Colombia—Highlights of Its Spanish Colonial Heritage. USA, 2013
Travel, Research and Teaching in Guatemala and Mexico—In Quest of the Pre-Columbian Heritage, Volume I—Guatemala, Volume II—Mexico. USA, 2013
A Portrait of Brazil in the Twentieth Century—The Universe of the "Literatura de Cordel." USA, 2013
Fifty Years of Research on Brazil—A Photographic Journey. USA, 2013
Travel and Teaching in Portugal and Spain - A Photographic Journey. USA, 2014

Professor Curran lives in Mesa, Arizona, and spends part of the year in Colorado. He is married to Keah Runshang Curran and they have a daughter Kathleen who lives in Albuquerque, New Mexico. Her documentary film Greening the Revolution was shown most recently at the Sonoma Film Festival. Katie was named "Best Female Director" at the Film Festival in Oaxaca, Mexico. The author's e-mail address: profmark@asu.edu
His website: http://www.currancordelconnection.com